MISSION POSSIBLE
GOALS GUIDE

4-18-2?

D1306332

MISSION POSSIBLE GOALS GUIDE

A 40-Day Plan to Making Each Moment Count

Tim Tebow

with A. J. Gregory

WATERBROOK

MISSION POSSIBLE GOALS GUIDE

All Scripture quotations, unless otherwise indicated, are taken from the (NASB®) New American Standard Bible®, copyright © 1960, 1971, 1977, 1995, 2020 by the Lockman Foundation. Used by permission. All rights reserved. (www.lockman.org). Scripture quotations marked (MSG) are taken from The Message, copyright © 1993, 2002, 2018 by Eugene H. Peterson. Used by permission of NavPress, represented by Tyndale House Publishers. All rights reserved. Scripture quotations marked (NKJV) are taken from the New King James Version®. Copyright © 1982 by Thomas Nelson. Used by permission. All rights reserved.

Copyright © 2022 by Timothy R. Tebow

All rights reserved.

Published in the United States by WaterBrook, an imprint of Random House, a division of Penguin Random House LLC.

WATERBROOK® and its deer colophon are registered trademarks of Penguin Random House LLC.

Some brief quotes in this work originally appeared in *Mission Possible,* copyright © 2022 by Timothy R. Tebow, published in the United States by WaterBrook, an imprint of Random House, a division of Penguin Random House LLC, in 2022.

LIBRARY OF CONGRESS CATALOGING-IN-PUBLICATION DATA
Names: Tebow, Tim, author. | Gregory, A. J., author.
Title: Mission possible goals guide : a 40-day plan to making each moment count / Tim Tebow with A.J. Gregory.
Description: First edition. | [Colorado Springs] : WaterBrook, [2022] | Includes bibliographical references.
Identifiers: LCCN 2021040750 | ISBN 9780593194058 (paperback) | ISBN 9780593194065 (ebook)
Subjects: LCSH: Time management. | Time—Psychological aspects. | Self-management (Psychology) | Success—Psychological aspects.
Classification: LCC BF637.T5 T43 2022 | DDC 650.1/1—dc23
LC record available at https://lccn.loc.gov/2021040750

Printed in the United States of America on acid-free paper

waterbrookmultnomah.com

1st Printing

First Edition

Interior book design by Virginia Norey

SPECIAL SALES Most WaterBrook books are available at special quantity discounts when purchased in bulk by corporations, organizations, and special-interest groups. Custom imprinting or excerpting can also be done to fit special needs. For information, please email specialmarketscms@penguinrandomhouse.com.

CONTENTS

CONTENTS

INTRODUCTION

WELCOME TO THIS FORTY-DAY JOURNEY OF LEARN-
ing how to live mission possible—achieving a life that makes a difference and leaves a legacy. I am so excited you have decided to join me on
this adventure.

In the great design of life, God created us to love and serve Him and
other people. We do this by using our gifts, talents, and resources, even
the seasons we find ourselves in, to shine light in our own unique ways.
In doing this, we help make our lives count. We leave marks on this world
by building lives that reach beyond ourselves. That is what really matters.

For the next forty days, I'm going to walk right beside you as you dig
deep and navigate what it looks like for *you* to live a life of purpose, passion, and significance. I designed this workbook to give you practical
tactics, a framework for understanding, and the confidence to live with
meaning. It's simply a guide.

You can have purpose without needing to have answers to all your
questions. You can find meaning where you are right now. You can live
with significance even if your level of success is not in tune with what
culture has defined it to be or where you might like to see it right now. It
will take work and grit, but you can do it!

Before you dig in, here is what you need to know.

What You Can Expect

THIS WORKBOOK IS BROKEN DOWN AS FOLLOWS:

Prelude	Days 1–3	Prepare for What's to Come
Module 1	Days 4–8	Unlock Your Purpose
Module 2	Days 9–13	Pursue Your Passion
Module 3	Days 14–18	Get Comfortable Being Uncomfortable
Module 4	Days 19–23	Get Locked In
Module 5	Days 24–28	Strain and Strive
Module 6	Days 29–33	Build Bridges
Module 7	Days 34–38	Consider Your Character
Postlude	Days 39–40	Bring It Home

We'll tackle such topics as how to find the inner drive to go all in, dismiss distractions, build better relationships, leverage discomfort and challenges, and learn key principles to develop better character—all things that lead us to living with purpose and creating lives that count.

How to Make Full Use of This Guide

TAKE NOTES, AS MANY AS YOU CAN! WRITE DOWN thoughts, ideas, dreams, goals—*anything* that comes to mind that has anything to do with living a mission-possible life. You may realize you have habits that need to change or negative mindsets that need to be detonated. Write these down, even if they do not seem to relate to the topic of the day. My purpose for coaching you through this process is not just for you to systemically follow this book day by day (although, obviously, that makes sense). My bigger purpose is for you to live a life that counts. So, if you think of something—anything—that will help you do that, write it down!

(By the way, there is enough room in this workbook to jot notes down, but consider using an app on your phone or a journal to have more space.)

Each "day" offers application exercises and reflection questions. The best thing you can do for yourself is to be honest. Take your time and think through each question. There are no right or wrong answers. Don't fill in the questions based on what you think others would want you to say. Answer them from your own heart.

Although I have structured this workbook to be completed in forty days, you can take longer. Go at your own pace. Do what works for you. If you need to skip a day and simmer on what you learned the day before, take that pause.

One more thing: you can come back to this guide anytime. As you continue to grow in your life and experience change, you may find it helpful to revisit certain modules or exercises. Some answers may even change. That's how it should be, because we change as we grow.

Speaking of change, I am excited to see growth begin to unfold in your life. You are here right now because you have already made a choice to grow—to refuse to be stuck in a matrix of meaningless days. You are choosing to bring new intention to your daily life. I'm here to help. Let's position your mind, your soul, and your spirit for impact. Let's start today to make your life count. I'll be right with you, every step of the way.

Let's do this!

PRELUDE

Prepare for What's to Come

Before we can craft lives that count, it is important to do some inner work. We need to call out what is not working right now.

What is holding you back from living a mission-possible life?

What fears have you not faced?

Let's work together for the next three days to do some inner excavating and unearth what is keeping you from living mission possible.

Day 1

WASTE-FREE ZONE

BEFORE IT WAS CLOSED IN 2012, BRAZIL'S JARDIM Gramacho was one of the world's largest garbage landfills. At 321 acres, it was the size of 243 American football fields! Every day around seven thousand tons of garbage (that's the weight of more than one hundred Boeing 757 airplanes) from the Rio de Janeiro metro area arrived. And then these discarded items entered a new life.[1]

Unofficially, the landfill had become a jobsite for scavengers, *catadores* in Portuguese, a community of men and women who salvaged the trash for recyclable materials. While Jardim Gramacho was still in operation, about three thousand catadores worked on the dump, wading knee deep in a sea of rotting food, busted-up glass, personal-care products, and just about every other type of garbage you can think of.[2] But for those picking through the heaps, there were occasional rewards. The catadores fished out two hundred tons of recyclable goods each day to sell to recyclers. This brings vivid meaning to the saying "One person's trash is another person's treasure."

The catadores lived and worked in garbage. It was the source of their livelihood and even their sustenance. They used or sold whatever they found. They ate nearly expired food spoiling under the hot sun. They hauled broken furniture to furnish their homes. Clothing too. They grabbed strangers' shampoo bottles and toothpaste tubes to use the last dollops of product. Even though it breaks my heart that those people lived that way, I am also in awe at their ability to have seen what others could not. In their economy, *nothing* was wasted.

God is not limited to overseeing a landfill in Brazil. However, He has a similar value for what others consider garbage. *Nothing* goes to waste in His economy if it is turned over to Him. When you base the trajectory of your life in not only who you are but whose you are, you can be confident knowing He's got your plan and purpose in control.

In this moment, you might feel hesitant about living fully mission driven. Your reluctance might stem from guilt or shame or regret from mistakes you have made or decisions that did not pan out to your benefit. Maybe life is not what you once hoped it would be. Maybe you're afraid of going all in and living a mission-possible life because, well, what if you mess up? What if you go left when God is leading you to make a right turn? What if you take a step in the wrong direction?

So many attitudes and beliefs hold us back. At times, I'm plagued by the fear I'll waste my life or that I won't fully use what God has given me for His purposes. It could be why I'm a super intense guy who's always operating in a state of urgency. (I am trying to chill a bit. I promise!) I need to remind myself that I am still a human being and that God is still God. I have to remember that even though my mission unfolds through my desires, my efforts, and my hard work, the Bible says that my times are in His hands (see Psalm 31:15).

There have been periods in my life when I felt God prompting me to do something. Sometimes it was naturally reinforced, like an opportunity that ended up with a great outcome. Other times it wasn't so great. Still other times it was just unclear what had happened. Also, although I try to take on every day with meaning and make each twenty-four-hour zone count, sometimes I'm tired, or I spend my day putting out fires, or what ends up being best is simply spending a day with my mom or dad. Even when I make a mistake or am wrong about something, I can look back and say with certainty that God has not wasted anything in my life that I have turned over to Him. And knowing that truth in the depths of my spirit, I am able to live a mission-possible life.

Before you dive deeper, I want you to try to put some things to rest. What attitudes or beliefs are holding you back from living mission possible? Shame from a past mistake? Feelings of unworthiness? Discouragement? Maybe you have been so overwhelmed with the responsibilities of life that you can't see beyond just treading water. Whatever it is, I promise you something: God does not want you to waste your life. And if you give Him what is holding you back right now, He will use whatever you give Him for His glory and to make a difference.

What internal attitudes or beliefs are getting in the way of you living a life that counts? Be as specific as you can.

_____

_____

_____

_____

_____

God will use *every* opportunity, even the broken and incomplete parts of your life, if you let Him. He will recycle them into something purposeful.

Look at that list. Think about it. Try to consider how these things have held you back in your life, and understand that you can move past them. I want you to end this time today by writing down truth-busting affirmations to counter what you've written down on the previous page. For example, if you think you're too old to live mission possible, write down someone you know who is of more mature years and is living each day with purpose. If you're in a season of life that's been abnormal or unpredictable, remind yourself that you can do hard things and be adaptive. If your expectations have been deflated and your hope for making a difference has really thinned out, tell yourself the truth that there is never a good time to give up. Use the space below to complete this exercise.

Holdbacks	Affirmations
1. _____	1. _____
2. _____	2. _____
3. _____	3. _____

Be encouraged knowing that when you give Him permission, your Father in heaven above is collecting all the pieces of your life and using them to produce an artful and legacy-producing masterpiece.

> *Everything in your past is preparation for something in your future. God wastes nothing!*
> —MARK BATTERSON, *Chase the Lion*

Day 2

SURRENDER: IT'S A GOOD THING

IN OUR CULTURE, THE WORD *SURRENDER* OFTEN has a negative connotation. At face value, the word conjures up negative images of waving a white flag, giving up, failure to overcome challenges, even defeat. *Surrender? Never!* It seems like an act of submission that we should avoid at all costs.

Winston Churchill, in one of the most iconic speeches of the twentieth century, rallied support from his fellow citizens and neighboring allies when he proclaimed, "We shall go on to the end. . . . We shall fight on the beaches, we shall fight on the landing grounds, we shall fight in the fields and in the streets, we shall fight in the hills; we shall never surrender."[3] We feel so inspired when we hear Churchill's determination. And rightly so! On the battlefield, surrender is the one thing you want to avoid at all costs. Why would you want to give up your keys to the fortress?

But *surrender* isn't always a dirty word. In some cases, it requires a unique perspective and special strength. It's not about giving up; it's about yielding control. In many ways, surrender looks more like victory than like failure.

In a spiritual context, we must embrace surrender. In order to live mission-driven lives, our priorities must be in order. The first step is surrendering our lives—our wants and preferences and even our steps—to God.

Reread that last sentence: "The first step is surrendering our lives—our wants and preferences and even our steps—to God." Take a breath.

What comes to mind when you hear yourself say those words out loud? Do they make you excited? Does your chest start to tighten? Write your answers down.

_____

_____

_____

_____

Many of us fear surrender because it's unknown. We fear surrender because it means we have no control. To whom or to what are we surrendering? Do we want to risk our lives, our dreams, our goals in the hands of something or someone other than ourselves, who may not have our best interests in mind?

I've found that surrender to God frightens many people. It causes them to stay stuck and refuse to let go of what is really a false sense of control over their lives. Rather than trusting that God knows best, we get this knot in our bellies and worry that God is going to make us do the one thing we've never wanted to do—such as spend the next thirty years in an impoverished community in a tropical climate without air-conditioning. We worry that God will pull the plug on the dreams, plans, and goals we've worked hard to accomplish.

Let me be honest with you. I don't know what God will do in your life. I don't know what He will ask of you (and I don't have the answers to those same questions in my own life). But this is what I know: I trust Him a lot more than I trust myself. I know I'm surrendering my present and my future to the God who is a much better driver of the ship than I am.

Remember whom you are surrendering to. You are not surrendering to an authoritarian figure waiting to exploit or abuse you on a twisted power trip. You are not giving your life over to a dictator who wants a robot as a soldier. Jesus paid the biggest price for you: His very own life. This speaks volumes of His character, of His great love for you. You can trust God because He gave up His best, His only Son, for you.

Have you ever lived fully surrendered? What did that mean or look like for you?

_____

_____

_____

_____

When you learn the fundamentals of a mission-possible life (that God loves you, that you are purposefully and uniquely made, and that

He has a plan for your life), the word *surrender* loses its negative connotations. And when you embrace those fundamentals, you're positioning yourself for a mission-possible life.

> *Surrender is like a fish finding the current*
> *and going with it.*
> —MARK NEPO,
> *"The Difference Between Acceptance and Surrender"*

Day 3

FACE THE FEAR

IN 2020, THE SECURITY FIRM ADT CONDUCTED A nationwide report on each state's most-searched phobia.[4] The most-googled fear in the United States at the time was anthropophobia, the fear of other people. It made up 22 percent of the search volume and increased five times compared to the year before. I'm sure COVID-19 had at least something to do with this growing fear of one another. The fear of being alone was another highly searched phobia that increased compared to prior years. In fact, it tripled since 2019 and in 2020 took first place in the states of Indiana, Minnesota, and Missouri. Florida's most-searched phobia was the fear of germs. In California, the phobia that topped all others was the fear of social media. I'm serious! Apparently, *that's a thing.* In New York, it was the fear of intimacy. In Massachusetts? The fear of failure. Think how much each of those says about our values and internal worlds.

Whether we're panic stricken by another human being, social media, or public speaking (which is another popular fear that, according to some studies, lands even higher on the fear factor scale than death!),[5] fear is a natural part of human life. Like common insects. No matter how clean your house is or how good of an exterminator you have, eventually you are going to run across an ant, a fly, a spider, or a few of some other crawlies.

And you know what? That's not bad! Most bugs are part of a healthy ecosystem. They may make some of us uncomfortable, but they are here because they have a job to do. Fear is the same. It isn't going away. In fact, fear is part of our survival mechanism—it belongs. Fear helps us be aware of danger and threats and triggers our fight-or-flight response. It's when fear shifts into overdrive that it becomes a problem. Not trying because we're afraid to fail or fearful of what others may think can paralyze us. Excessive fear keeps us toxically rooted in a place of worrying and overanalyzing. When we are in that unhealthy space, we're not living mission forward; we're merely existing.

Fear cripples people. It makes us to want to curl up in the fetal position and do nothing. In my experience, it is the number one obstacle that keeps us from living to our fullest God-given potential. Yet even when, for whatever reason, we are gripped tight in what can feel like fear's paralyzing clutch, we still have a choice: Do we allow it to rule over our lives and abandon the purpose that God has placed in us, or do we reach forward, trembling on the inside a little, palms sweaty, yet trusting more in God's character than in our emotions?

As you work through this coaching guide, I want you to start by being honest with yourself. Before we get to the place of uncovering potential, sometimes we have to excavate the soil in which we did not flourish, or maybe revisit the places we were too afraid to plant or even break ground.

In the space on the next page, take some time to list ways you have been affected by fear in the past. Perhaps you still carry shame, guilt, or regret caused by it. Or maybe fear has led to missed opportunities for you. Whatever the case may be, jot it down. Remember, shining light on your past produces growth.

_____

_____

_____

_____

_____

Sometimes the best way to process our fear is to face it head-on. Don't worry—you won't be forced to spend the night in your bed with a family of spiders.

1. I'd like you to visualize yourself living a mission-possible life to your fullest potential. Now carefully consider what could go wrong. Imagine that scenario; then write down the top two or three things that make you afraid. In other words, *What is the worst that can happen?*

_____

_____

_____

_____

2. Look at what you've written down. Spend a few minutes processing your answers. Write down what you could do if one or all of those things happened. For example, you may fear a financial loss or the loss of time. You might fear being embarrassed after putting yourself out there. You could be afraid that a goal or dream of yours may need to be sidelined, either temporarily or permanently. If that were to happen as you pursue a mission-possible life, consider shifting your focus to what you will *gain* instead—a deeper relationship with God, plus, when you surround yourself with like-minded people who are living centered on God and others, they can encourage you on your journey. If the worst happens, what positive outcomes may result that would not have happened otherwise?

_____

_____

_____

_____

3. Now let's put aside the what-if, worst-case scenarios and focus on what could happen if you chose to live a mission-possible life to your fullest potential. What two future positive life developments can you most look forward to?

_____

_____

A friend of mine once said that the opposite of faith isn't doubt; it's fear. Faith overcomes fear because the object of your faith, Jesus, overcame the world. This doesn't mean you'll stop asking questions. This doesn't mean you won't have doubts. This doesn't mean you won't encounter fear. It means trusting the character of the Creator of this universe is a better choice than crumbling under pressure or doing nothing because you're scared. Don't let fear cripple you from making a decision, pursuing a passion, or seizing an opportunity. Let faith lead the way.

Inaction breeds doubt and fear. Action breeds confidence and courage. If you want to conquer fear, don't sit home and think about it. Go out and get busy!
—DALE CARNEGIE, *The 5 Essential People Skills*

MODULE 1

Unlock Your Purpose

When you begin to live with intentionality, you find meaning even in what you normally may consider ordinary. So, for the next five days, we're going to tap into the fundamentals of creating a mission-possible life.

The first step?

Recognizing there is a purpose in all things.

Day 4

PURPOSE IS EVERYWHERE

AS 1665 CAME TO A CLOSE, THE SURVIVORS OF THE Great Plague in England were looking forward to a new year, much like many of us did after the pandemic of 2020. The year 1666 started out unscathed by tragedy until September 2, when a fire broke out near the London Bridge.[1] It had been a hot and dry summer, so the oak and timber homes were primed to catch and spread fire. By September 4, half of London was covered in flames. When the Great Fire was finally put out two days later, over four-fifths of the city was destroyed. London had morphed into an unrecognizable mountain of rubbish and ashes. Around a hundred thousand people were left homeless.

One victim of the Great Fire was St. Paul's Cathedral, which had stood on Ludgate Hill since 604. Famed architect Sir Christopher Wren was assigned to design and rebuild the cathedral. It's said that during the reconstruction, Wren watched three bricklayers who were working on a scaffold. He asked each man the same question: "What are you doing?" Their responses varied.

The first said, "I am laying bricks."

The second replied, "I am building a wall."

The third answered, "I am building a great cathedral for God."[2]

I'm not sure if Wren actually asked the bricklayers that question, but let the point sink in. They were all, in fact, laying bricks to build a wall. But the third bricklayer expressed a meaningful and long-term vision for his labor. Same task, different purposes.

Sometimes it's not about changing what we do; it's about changing how we see what we do.

So let's take inventory of your life. In the first column, write down how you spend a typical twenty-four-hour day, listing your activities from the time you wake up until the time you go to bed. In the next column, write down the first thing that comes to your mind concerning that activity's purpose. Why do you do it? Spend a few more minutes really thinking about the greater purpose. Then write that down in the final column. This exercise is intended to help you identify purpose, both immediate and greater, in what you might overlook as ordinary.

Activity	Purpose	Greater Purpose
Wake and exercise	Lose weight/ Get toned	To get in shape so I can be a fit and healthy parent and lead my children in a healthy lifestyle

Activity	Purpose	Greater Purpose

As Christians, we have purpose because Jesus died for us and was raised from the dead. Through Him, we have new life. And because of this sacrifice, we live to glorify God. Life on earth is also a journey to become more and more like Jesus. We seek to know Him. We also honor Him with our gifts, time, resources, dreams, and plans.

Usually, it is in our moments of crisis or on a milestone birthday that we start to ache with regret or wallow in misery because we're stuck in what feels like a cycle of meaninglessness. We work for a paycheck. With packed calendars and stacked responsibilities, it feels like we are parenting just to keep our kids alive, fed, clothed, and housed. We maintain relationships through texts rather than deep conversations. We invest in our spiritual lives by skimming through devotionals for five minutes in the morning, if we're lucky. Whether we're encumbered by the tyranny of the urgent or run down by the rote, something is missing. Am I speaking directly to you?

I want to ask something of you. It may seem like a strange exercise at first, but stay with me. Instead of getting to your sixtieth birthday and wondering what you've done with your life, let's pretend it is your sixtieth birthday *now*!

The table is set. Decorations are hung. Balloons are on display. Gifts are stacked in a corner. Guests have arrived and are ready to celebrate—you! A good friend has arranged for three important people in your life to share a few words in honor of this special day. Now think of who those three people might be—maybe a parent, a spouse, a best friend, a mentor, a boss, a coach, or a professor. Write down what you would like these three individuals to say about who you are and what you've done in your life thus far.

This exercise is intended to help you envision the person you'd like to become and help build your mission statement in the next chapter.

Person #1: _____

Person #2: _____

Person #3: _____

We may not lay bricks to reconstruct an ancient cathedral, but we are each playing a role of some sort in this life. If you're a student, are you just reading books, or are you studying for a diploma? Are you getting educated on a subject with which you can make positive change? In the divine master plan, purpose is planted in our DNA. We may not know exactly what that purpose is, but it is automatically present in the present. Let's not waste or miss it!

> *My question—that which at the age of fifty brought me to the verge of suicide—was the simplest of questions, lying in the soul of every man: it was a question without an answer to which one cannot live. It was: "What will come of what I am doing today or tomorrow? What will come of my whole life? . . . Why should I live, why wish for anything, or do anything?" It can also be expressed thus: "Is there any meaning in my life that the inevitable death awaiting me does not destroy?"*
>
> —LEO TOLSTOY, *A Confession*

Day 5

LIVE ON PURPOSE
BY DEFINING YOUR MISSION

WE ARE GOD THE FATHER'S CHILDREN, SPECIAL, adopted into His family. And in having this wonderful privilege, we get to praise Him with our lives and tell others about His love. That's the root of the answer to the question "What is my purpose?"

In your own words, write down what your purpose is as a child of God. After you've done this, read aloud what you wrote. Repeat it a few times. Write it on a sticky note and post it somewhere you can see it. If you're feeling ambitious, memorize it. Whenever you're feeling lost or unsure or just not feeling anything at all, you can ground yourself by repeating your purpose as a believer.

_____

_____

_____

_____

_____

Now let's tackle this even a bit more personally. What does living out this purpose look like for you and me? Does it have to do with where we go to school or live or what career we choose? I like to think the first way to cover this ground is to create a personal mission statement. If you've read *Mission Possible,* you may have done this already. Awesome! If needed, see if you can make a few adjustments. If you haven't made one yet, let's get started.

But wait, there's something we need to do first. I want you to think back on a time when you experienced a deep sense of purpose. Maybe you were a teenager on your first mission trip or were playing in a tournament, hoping to clinch the championship title. Now write your answers to the following questions:

What was I doing?

_____

_____

_____

_____

_____

Who was I doing it for?

_____

_____

_____

_____

_____

What was the outcome?

_____

_____

_____

_____

Think about how it made you feel. Were you flooded with a sense of peace or clarity? Did you feel fulfilled? Don't overthink it. Jot down one-word answers, whatever comes to mind. Recalling this event will spark certain emotions. And even though I don't usually place too much emphasis on feelings (they often betray us, after all), for the sake of this exercise, re-feeling them might help as you begin to think of a mission statement for your life. Complete the following sentence.

When I had a sense of purpose, I felt . . .

_____

_____

_____

_____

Let's get back to the present. My mission statement, and the one we use for our foundation, is "to bring faith, hope, and love to those needing a brighter day in their darkest hour of need."[3] We want to fight for people who can't fight for themselves. We do this by serving orphans, people with special needs, and others. When I don't feel necessarily driven or focused or psyched, I think about this mission statement. And when I do, it gives me the strength to crush whatever task lies before me.

A personal mission statement will help you take action. It addresses what you do and for whom. Flip back to yesterday's assignment. You were asked to write three speeches celebrating yourself at age sixty. Look back at that exercise and notice how it answered the following questions:

What do I value?

_____

_____

_____

_____

What legacy do I want to leave?

_____

_____

_____

_____

Who do I want to help and how?

_____

_____

_____

_____

After reading the following purposes for and tips about mission statements, use the answers to yesterday's exercise to begin writing your own personal mission statement on the next page.

_____

_____

_____

_____

_____

_____

_____

_____

What a Mission Statement Does
• It provides a framework for how you want to live. • It expresses your values and priorities. • It determines your best self. • It motivates you to stay the course.

Mission Statement Tips

- Focus on what you want, not what you don't want.
- Stay positive and self-affirming.
- Keep it short, simple, and concise—preferably, a sentence or two at most.
- It doesn't have to be in complete sentences.
- Make the statement sound like you. Don't craft a sentence you think would make your boss happy or your mentor happy. Be you.

Congratulations! You've just completed one of the first steps to living on purpose. I'm excited to see what this week holds for you.

There is nothing more freeing than abandoning your own mission and joining the everyday mission of God.
—DUSTIN WILLIS AND AARON COE, *Life on Mission*

Day 6

LOSE THE EXCUSES

I REMEMBER PLAYING WITH THE BRONCOS AGAINST the Patriots one night in January 2012 when it felt like the temperature was below zero. We were getting slaughtered by New England. At the beginning of the third quarter, we were down 42–7. I'll never forget getting tackled and hitting the ground, crushed by the weight of several Patriots piling on top of me. Upon impact, I felt my chest snap. I'd find out later I had broken multiple bones in my chest. When I got up, I could feel the broken bones shifting and popping. The pain was excruciating. But I knew this was a chance for me to make a statement for my team.

See, it's not just about showing up when you're winning. It's also about fighting when it's bleak. It's about rallying when you're getting blown out and there is no probable chance of a comeback. I played the rest of the game, every single snap. Now, I admit that staying in the game probably made my injuries worse, but I was determined to stick it out and fight. If I'm going down, I would like to be someone who would make the choice to go down fighting.

You don't need to break some bones to push through pain and get the job done. Sometimes it's just about getting uncomfortable to do what's right or what matters or what you set out to do.

Living mission possible isn't easy. There are plenty of excuses that can get in your way and stop the momentum. It's always fun and exciting to start something new. But after a while, the enthusiasm can wane, making it feel harder or even rote. Sometimes a new routine can throw us off, or an unexpected shift, such as a pandemic, demands we rethink the way we've always operated or managed our lives. Or maybe we're experiencing the hard hits of a traumatic experience, or life is just not working out as we had planned. When these things occur, mission-possible living can feel like playing ball with a few cracked ribs.

When's the last time you achieved a goal or broke through a barrier because of a "no matter what it takes" attitude? Write down that experience, including the obstacles that impeded your progress. What was it that you believed in so much that helped you push past these challenges?

_____

_____

_____

_____

_____

_____

I wonder how many times we negotiate our way out of mission-possible lives or, really, out of any goals we set for ourselves. We know where we want to go, we know what we want to do, but it's so easy to let excuses stunt our growth. *I didn't get up early enough because I stayed up too late. . . . It's just not a good time right now. . . . Maybe next week will be better. . . . If I can't give it my best now, why even try?*

Spend time thinking about the past six to twelve months. What are three important things you wanted to do to better yourself or cultivate more purpose into your life but for which you found yourself making excuses and not following through? Following the example below, list the activities or goals and provide the excuse you gave for each.

Goal	Excuse
Wake up earlier to meditate and read the Bible	I'd stay up late binge-watching shows and would be too tired to get up early
1. _____	1. _____
2. _____	2. _____
3. _____	3. _____

Look at these excuses. There might be a legitimate one in there, a life-changing circumstance such as loss or trauma. But I have a feeling there's at least one that you don't want to keep excusing.

When we face excuses head-on, they begin to lose their power. And little by little, day by day, a new kind of living begins to awaken—a mission-possible way of living. We start to realize we can do the hard things we never believed we could. When you make this choice, you'll begin to notice changes, small at first, then ones that make a lasting impact. And you believe you can finish what you started, a little battered and bruised in the end maybe, but achieving what you set out to accomplish.

A man can fail many times, but he isn't a failure until he begins to blame somebody else.

—John Burroughs

Day 7

DETERMINE YOUR NONNEGOTIABLES

LONG AFTER WE HAD ESTABLISHED THE TIM TEBOW Foundation's mission statement, I knew we could depict our mission with even more specific direction. This is what led me to create our organization's nonnegotiables.

Nonnegotiables are the values, principles, actions, and beliefs that you will refuse to go against in life. They are driving forces for personal growth. They are constant and never compromised. Tim determine what you want your life to represent and how you want to live it out. They also help sustain and propel your mission forward. They are essential. In some arenas, they're called core values.

I take nonnegotiables seriously. For me, they are deeply rooted beliefs I can never negotiate on, no matter what. Here are a few general nonnegotiables:

Exercise

Trust God in all things

Express gratitude to God and others

Nurture relationships

24 hours screen-free during week	1 day a week off social media
Meditation	Bible study and prayer
Keep my word	Deliver servant leadership
Focus on faith rather than feelings	Spend quality time with family
Charitable giving	Generosity
Integrity	Influence my community

Here's a peek into what, after much prayer and reflection, we at our foundation decided were our nonnegotiables. (These are also my personal nonnegotiables.)

1. **We are believers.** We are believers in a big God, in Jesus, in the ability to create change, in the truth that we matter and that we are all here on purpose.

2. **Everyone matters. We are all image bearers.** We all have worth and value. We get to serve God, not play God. We don't get to choose who matters.

3. **We are on a rescue mission.** When we put the word *rescue* before *mission*, it creates a sense of urgency. A rescue mission doesn't take place in a year, nor is it based on our own timelines; it's based on the timelines of those who are abandoned, lost, or hurting.

4. **There's power when we unite.** When we come together, we can accomplish more. We want to create an army of people

who are willing to stand on the line to bring light and push back darkness. And when we believe that the mission is more important than the individual credit, lives will be changed.

5. **Don't forget.** We will always remember the moments that changed our lives. I can never forget Sherwin, the boy with special needs whom I met in the Philippines when I was fifteen who inspired me to start the foundation.

Let's kick off the basics first. Answer the following questions to start crafting your own set of nonnegotiables:

What standards do you need to set to feel present in your life?

_____

_____

_____

_____

_____

_____

_____

What beliefs will you refuse to back down from, no matter what?

_____

_____

_____

_____

_____

What kinds of experiences do you need in order to feel alive, purpose filled, and at peace?

_____

_____

_____

_____

_____

What motivates and fulfills you?

_____

_____

_____

_____

_____

_____

Look at what you've just written. Use that material to write down five nonnegotiables you want to live by. They can be as big or small as you like, but they must align with your mission. They can be statements like the one we chose for our foundation, or they can be one-word values such as courage, confidence, compassion, service, and loyalty.

You may wish to refer to the different categories listed on the next page as a reference to give you some ideas of where to begin.

_____

_____

_____

_____

_____

_____

While I can't establish your nonnegotiables for you, consider your top ones wrapped around your identity as a child of God. Write them here.

_____

_____

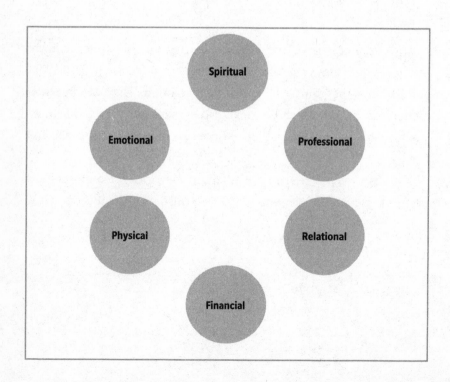

When you couple your nonnegotiables with your mission statement, you invite significance and purpose to the story of your life. You begin to find satisfaction in every day, even the ones that seem trivial or uneventful. Having nonnegotiables and a mission statement helps us make the best use of our time. While none of us will live out our missions perfectly, being committed to them gives our lives more meaning and helps us stay the course rather than just trying to get by.

Strong convictions precede great actions.
—JAMES FREEMAN CLARKE, *The Columbian Speaker*

Day 8

START RIGHT

THERE IS NO TIME LIKE THE START OF EACH NEW day. One of the easiest ways to unlock purpose in your day is to craft a morning ritual. This means you stop tapping the snooze button on your watch or phone until you're already six minutes late. Whenever you do start your day, make sure you have time to start *right*. Night owls, stay with me! I'm not saying you have to give up your late evenings and start rising way before the sun starts shining. But you may have some tweaking to do. And, morning people, it's not enough to just get up. You have to make the most of a good beginning.

Think about it. How you spend the morning is going to carry over into the rest of your day. If you're rushed and stressed before you head out the door or open your laptop in your home office, that feeling is likely going to stick with you for the rest of the day. And the last thing on your mind is how you are going to tackle your day guided by your mission statement and nonnegotiables.

Benefits of a Morning Routine

- **develops healthy habits**
- **increases productivity**
- **decreases stress**
- **sets the tone for the rest of the day**
- **reminds you of your priorities**

For me, time spent in prayer and reading the Bible is a must. I admit, I'm more of a night owl, so most of my in-depth spiritual studying is spent at night, when my mental productivity is at its peak. But this doesn't mean I don't try to connect with God when I first wake up. I've learned how important this is to do. I want my initial thoughts, even before my feet hit the floor, to be centered on thanking God for a new day and giving it to Him.

How you decide to spend your morning is up to you. It also depends on what your work schedule is, if you have little ones, or any number of things. What's important is developing some sort of ritual that allows you to be intentional about starting your day rather than letting the day rule your beginning.

Let's start by creating a NOT-To-Do List. We each have tasks that we do, consciously or subconsciously, that tend to nibble away at our energy and time and serve zero purpose, other than causing our blood pressure to skyrocket. These include scrolling through social media or checking news apps. Maybe there are things we do that we don't have to necessarily do right then, such as check work email. Before you start setting up (and tweaking as you go) an effective morning routine, I want you to think about what you probably need to stop doing in the morning.

Think about your typical morning, from the time you wake up until you begin your day at school, at work, in the home with little ones, outside the home, or working remotely. Write down the details of your regimen here:

_____

_____

_____

_____

_____

_____

_____

_____

_____

_____

Foundational Elements of a Morning Routine

- **Spend quiet time with God.**
- **Do what's important to you.**
- **Keep it simple.**
- **Make it manageable. It can be fifteen minutes or one hour.**
- **Make necessary tweaks. If something isn't working, instead of giving up the whole routine, just make a small change.**

Review what you jotted down. Now in the space below, list the things you do that take away from your goals, time, energy, or best self. (Be honest with yourself.) This is your NOT-To-Do List for mornings.

_____

_____

_____

_____

_____

Now create a revised morning ritual. It can be as detailed as you'd like, but I am going to challenge you to stick with it for at least the next thirty days. Don't rush through this process. Really think about it. Here are some ideas that you can incorporate into your routine:

Exercise	Journal
Recite affirmations	Read a book
Learn a word	Read a poem
Spend quality time with kids	Make breakfast
Stretch	Meditate
Make a goal list	Work on a crossword puzzle
Do a breathing exercise	Plan your day
Listen to a podcast	Make your bed (Hey, Navy Seals do it!)
Hydrate	Get some sun (Pull back those curtains and splash some sunlight over your face!)

Write down each activity and anticipate the amount of time it will take.

_____

_____

_____

_____

_____

_____

_____

_____

_____

_____

_____

_____

Benjamin Franklin made no secret of his morning ritual. He would often start his day by asking himself, *What good shall I do this day?* If you've never seen his daily routine (as listed in his autobiography), look it up![4] He rose early, planned his day, worked, read, ate well, stayed organized, reflected on his day, and got good sleep. That's worth imitating!

Setting up a morning ritual opens the door to starting the day ready to embark on a purpose-filled mission. Here's a thought: read your purpose, mission statement, or nonnegotiables (or all of the above) as part of your morning routine!

Give every day the chance
to become the most beautiful day of your life.
—MARK TWAIN

MODULE 2

Pursue Your Passion

Passion is an essential ingredient to making your life count. And it means a whole lot more than having a strong feeling or affection for something or somebody. It has to do with being willing to sacrifice for a greater purpose. Over the next five days, you're going to reframe your perspective of passion when it comes to learning, serving, and taking risks and see where it really fits in.

Day 9

FOLLOW YOUR PASSION?
THINK AGAIN

IF YOU'RE SITTING IN AN AUDIENCE LISTENING TO A commencement address, perusing motivational quotes on social media, or burying yourself in articles about innovative entrepreneurs such as Elon Musk and Steve Jobs, you'll probably come across this popular adage: "Find something you love to do and you'll never have to work a day in your life." Here's another spin on it: "Don't settle. Follow your passion."

Isn't that outright hypnotic? It immediately conjures images of creating your own jewelry line or jet-setting around the globe and starting your own travel vlog. Those are pretty cool things to do, and I won't discourage you from setting those goals if that's what you think a mission-possible life looks like. Although those quotes refer to our careers, there seems to be a bigger push for passion these days in all aspects of our lives.

A common complaint for couples who have been married for a long time is waning passion. The spark is gone. He doesn't get the goose bumps he used to when he holds his wife's hand. She doesn't get butterflies anymore when she looks at her husband from across the room. The magic has faded. The fireworks are long gone. Passion? What passion?

We talk about passion as though it's some mystical inner fire that activates within us naturally without any struggle or sweat. It's this burning desire that makes us do crazy things like swim across the ocean, battling frigid temperatures and raging waves, to proclaim our love for the one who has stolen our heart. We imagine passion will give us the stamina and endurance to work forty hours straight without interruption because—eureka!—we've begun to create something with brilliance and innovation that will change the world. After all, the dictionary defines *passion* as "any powerful or compelling emotion or feeling, as love or hate."[1] This is what passion means—and does—right?

Tomorrow we're going to dive into the origin and meaning of the word *passion*. Today we'll focus on our cultural perception of the word and how we have positioned it in our own lives.

I want you to spend a few minutes thinking about the word *passion* and how you have defined it. Write your definition in the space below and then answer the questions that follow.

_____

_____

Is passion sustainable? Why or why not?

_____

_____

_____

_____

_____

_____

Is passion necessary? Why or why not?

_____

_____

_____

_____

How do you see passion adding value to a mission-possible life?

_____

_____

_____

_____

_____

_____

What role does passion play in your work?

_____

_____

_____

_____

_____

What role does passion play in your relationships?

_____

_____

_____

_____

If you view passion as a strong emotion that compels excitement, promotes an inner drive, and is coupled with talent, read on. You may be shocked. Passion may have less to do with the above and more to do with the sweat, blood, and tears of living mission possible.

"Follow your passion" might be the worst advice you ever get. A 2018 study from psychologists at Stanford and Yale-NUS College examined whether our passions are hidden until we find them (a fixed theory) or something to be developed and nurtured (a growth theory).[2] It was determined that people who believe in the fixed theory of passion (the ones who embrace the "follow your passion" advice) had a distorted perception of passion. Believing that passion was something in them that just appeared made them more likely to give up when they faced challenges or roadblocks. They were also more likely to believe that pursuing their passion would be easy and that they would have limitless motivation in the process. Finding that wasn't true, they would become disillusioned and quit their pursuits.

Before we continue, think of a time when following your passion led you astray. What was the outcome? List two pieces of advice that you would tell your former self right before making the decision to follow your passion.

_____

_____

_____

The bottom line is that pursuing passion may not be the greatest tool for building a mission-possible life. Passion is not a magic bullet. Passion may be part of it, but passion in *Webster*'s terms is not the driving force that will help you fulfill a life of purpose.

However, when we begin to view passion in the right context, we begin to feel the weight of the word, in a fulfilling and challenging kind of way. Let's go there tomorrow.

> *Nothing great in the world*
> *has ever been accomplished without passion.*
> —GEORG WILHELM FRIEDRICH HEGEL, *The Philosophy of History*

Day 10

WHAT ARE YOU WILLING TO SACRIFICE FOR?

THE WORD *PASSION* WAS FIRST INTRODUCED TO the English language in the twelfth century to describe the sufferings of Christ between the night of the Last Supper and His death. *Passion* comes from the Latin root word *passio,* which means "suffering."[3] It wasn't until the fourteenth century that *passion* took on an emotional— and more sanitized—meaning. In our modern definition, *passion* is associated with strong affection or zeal.

I don't know many people today who would use *passion* and *suffering* in the same sentence. But as the word's origin reminds us, the two are connected. Which makes me wonder, can you be passionate about something and not be willing to suffer for it? Can you achieve the win without the training and the aches? Can you experience a loving relationship without sacrificing your preferences? Can you enjoy the beauty of the sunrise without rising at the crack of dawn? It seems that so many of us settle for less than mission possible because life is uncomfortable, uncertain, and at times unpleasant.

Home to seven of the world's ten largest glaciers,[4] the Bridger Wilderness sits within the Wind River Mountains in Wyoming. Alpine ponds and mountain lakes rest below rugged granite peaks that graze the clouds. It's a paradise for outdoor enthusiasts. But if you plan on enjoying this natural oasis by way of hiking, fishing, or camping, be prepared to battle the varying elements (snow, freezing temperatures or blazing heat depending on the season, high elevation, rocky trails, and pesky critters, to name a few). Comes with the territory, right? I mean that quite literally.

In 1996, the following comment cards were collected by the staff at this national park:[5]

- Trails need to be wider so people can walk while holding hands.
- Instead of a permit system or regulations, the Forest Service needs to reduce worldwide population growth to limit the number of visitors to wilderness.
- Ban walking sticks in wilderness. Hikers that use walking sticks are more likely to chase animals.
- Trail needs to be reconstructed. Please avoid building trails that go uphill.
- Too many bugs and leeches and spiders and spiderwebs. Please spray the wilderness to rid the area of these pests.
- Please pave the trails so they can be plowed of snow during the winter.
- Chairlifts need to be in some places so that we can get to wonderful views without having to hike to them.
- The coyotes made too much noise last night and kept me awake. Please eradicate these annoying animals.

- A small deer came into my camp and stole my jar of pickles. Is there a way I can get reimbursed?

Hilarious! But there's a deeper principle about human nature at play here. We want the view without the work, the glamour of living a life of passion without the suffering it takes to get there. We want nature as long as it's not too . . . natural.

It's not about choosing to suffer for suffering's sake. That's masochistic or stupid. Probably both. *Passion* in its original meaning is to suffer for the sake of someone else. Take Jesus, for instance. He didn't choose to suffer on the cross and die just because. He chose to be a sacrifice in order to take our place. He chose to suffer for the greater good of our salvation. He did it for a purpose. He did it because it was His mission.

Think about passion in this light and in the context of your mission statement and then answer the following.

What are you willing to suffer for? What great need do you see in the world today that you are willing to change or meet and, in the process, embrace hardship for in order to fulfill your mission?

_____

_____

_____

_____

_____

_____

This may sound pretty dramatic. I don't mean for you to envision yourself sacrificing your life for the plight of the world. Jesus already did that. Let's think about mission and passion more concretely. If your mission is to spread love in your community, passion can help arm you in that fight and prevent you from shying away from relational conflict. Passion will sustain you when your neighbor starts bad-mouthing your efforts, keeping you from calling it quits at the first sign of resistance.

I can't promise you that on the climb of a mission-possible life you'll get reimbursed for a jar of pickles a deer might have stolen, but hopefully your outdoor experience will far outweigh your loss of a few bucks.

Jesus, the author and finisher of our faith, who for the joy that was set before Him endured the cross, despising the shame, and has sat down at the right hand of the throne of God.

—HEBREWS 12:2, NKJV

Day 11

BE OPEN

I OFTEN THINK OF THIS SAYING: "WE MAKE A LIVING by what we get, but we make a life by what we give." When we have conversations about purpose and mission, I sense this undue pressure that many of us feel. We think we have this one thing we must do in this life or else we will lack the meaning and significance that we are destined for. We tend to overcomplicate simple things.

When we take it to the ground, one of the biggest action steps we can take in building lives of purpose and significance is to be open. You don't always have to have a particular passion for just one cause or group of people. It's more organic than that. Be open to serving others. Be open to seeing a need and meeting it. Be open to encouraging someone. Listen. Serve. Give. Love. In big ways? Sure. But don't forget the small ways. They matter too.

I like to think of three channels to do this:

1. **Open your eyes.** Slow down enough to observe what's happening around you. See the needs of others.

2. **Open your heart to love.** There are so many things in this life that can harden your spirit. But when you live each day softened by the power of love, you can allow love to enter you, change you, and therefore help change those around you.

3. **Open your hands to give.** We can live tightfisted, holding on to everything we have, whether our time, resources, talents, or generosity. Share whatever you have been given with those around you.

Use the following prompts and the scale on the next page to determine how open you are to recognizing the needs of others and reaching out. Then read the description that matches your score to reflect on how you can improve in this area.

- Do you listen for a friend who gives you a clue on the phone that he or she needs help?
- Do you take a break from doing a chore so you can hear your kid's story?
- Do you give up something in your schedule for somebody else?

Circle your score.

Completely blinded by self   Continually aware of
(thoughts/distractions/   the needs of others
agenda/schedule)

1   2   3   4   5   6   7   8   9   10

If You Circled 1–3

I wonder what keeps you from being aware of your environment. It could be a hyperactive tendency to be distracted or maybe you're in a rough season that demands your attention and energy and you're having a difficult time seeing outside your oxygen-depleting bubble. If you're loaded with distractions, it's time to sit down with yourself and, well, stop for a moment. Stop rushing. Be still. Pay more attention to the present moment. Find strategies to do this on a more consistent basis. Research tells us that being more mindful to the world around us (and I don't mean the world on social media) can improve our well-being. So take the time to look at someone's face. Notice your coworker or the barista who serves you every morning. Be kind. Spread joy.

If you're in a stressful season, I get it. It's hard to be aware of others during this time. I encourage you to do something that's personally helped me. Whenever I've gone through periods of feeling down, I'd visit the local hospital and spend time with sick children who needed a smile. Many times, while I hoped to bring them joy, they were the ones lifting my own spirit. It seems counterintuitive, but when we reach out to others in our own pain, we end up on the receiving end of joy.

If You Circled 4–6

I sense you have a spirit that's willing to be open to love and serve others. That's awesome! It could be that something is holding you back from acting on what you see. During the course of the day, you may notice someone who could use a person to talk to but you feel weird about approaching him or her, so you don't. Muster up courage next time and reach out. The biggest regret you'll have is not saying anything. As Susan Jeffers's book says, feel the fear and do it anyway.[6]

It could be that although your drive to make a difference is there, you're not sure where to start. Start small. Tackle your day with kindness—to everyone! Start at home, with your family or your roommate, or with the people you see on a regular basis. Send them encouraging texts. Buy them some flowers. Put their needs before your preferences. Show them mercy. You don't have to carry the burden of changing the world; you just have to spread some light right where you are.

If You Circled 7–9

You have an awareness of others around you and are likely doing what you can to reach out to those in need. I love that! Maybe it's time to stretch yourself a little further. Push yourself slightly out of your comfort zone. Maybe, if you're not already doing this, dig a little deeper into the problems you see, the ones that move you, in your sphere of influence. Maybe homelessness is a problem in your community. Could you volunteer in the local shelter or work with your local government to enact positive change? Perhaps it's time to reevaluate your financial situation. Maybe your spending habits could be adjusted so what you spend on what you definitely don't need could be spent on more useful resources, such as nonprofit organizations that are dear to you. I'm proud of your generous heart and know you can step it up even more!

If You Circled 10

Congratulations! Why on earth are you reading this book? You can give me some pointers! Seriously, email me! I don't know what you're doing, but you're doing something right. Bravo! Keep it up!

* * *

Whatever you scored, just remember, when you take the first steps by opening your eyes, your heart, and your hands, you begin to create a life of significance.

No act of kindness, no matter how small, is ever wasted.
—AESOP, *Aesop's Fables*

Day 12

MUSAR DRIVEN

ONE OF THE MOST DRIVEN PEOPLE I KNOW, IN AND OUT OF SPORTS, is my beautiful wife, Demi-Leigh. When I first met her in April 2018, she was several months into her reign as Miss Universe—something I knew absolutely nothing about! On our first date, I was not only blown away by the radiance of her smile and her sweet, humble spirit, but as we talked about life, I also found myself very attracted to her drive, ambition, and hunger to live out the mission that God has put on her heart.

One thing that really impressed me was how hard she worked to win Miss Universe 2017. For those of you who don't know, Miss Universe is a once-in-a-lifetime competitive event. Literally. You can only compete in it one time. So for Demi, after she won Miss South Africa (her home country) and had a chance to compete in Miss Universe, the challenge wasn't something she took lightly. She wanted to represent her country well and be the most prepared person on that stage.

In the months leading up to the competition, Demi sought out a professional pageant coach to help her with public speaking, hair and makeup, understanding politics and current events, and many other details that no one thinks about. She also asked her friends and family to speak only English to her. Why? Because her native language, Afrikaans, wasn't widely spoken and she felt that being able to speak clear English to communicate her message would give her the best shot at winning. Of course, this means she succeeded with English, her second language! She's amazing!

Demi is what I like to call "musar driven"!

What is *musar*, you ask?

Musar is an old Hebrew word that refers to the process of learning. It can be defined as training, discipline, instruction, and correction. The term occurs roughly fifty times in the Old Testament and is predominantly found in the book of Proverbs (thirty times).[7] It involves fatherly correction, moral discipline, and character development. Simply put, musar is how we grow and mature.

Throughout the Bible, there is high value placed on receiving musar. Wisdom is acquired through it, and those who refuse it are fools (see Proverbs 1:7; 12:1; 15:32–33). In pursuing passion, training and discipline are essential. They build skills and develop character. Being musar driven not only aids passion but also propels it forward.

Unfortunately, most people don't have this mindset. They're content with where they are in life. They reject feedback, take things personally, and aren't willing to find mentors. But not Demi. She desires growth. She wants others in her life to push her, train her, and teach her in order to maximize her God-given abilities. Not only did she seek musar during her pageant career, but she also continues to do so in all facets of life—spiritually, emotionally, physically, and relationally.

Musar is nonstop.

Once Demi made it to the highest level her industry had to offer, it would've been so easy for her to say, "I've made it. I know it all." But she doesn't say that. She continues to strive to improve herself every day.

Because of that drive, and for so many other reasons, she makes me a better person!

Being coachable requires zero talent. All it takes is making the decision to be teachable and efforts to learn. Go to your pastor, go to your teacher, go to your coach, and go to your boss—and listen to what they have to say. Don't just wait for correction to come to you. Go seek musar. If you're not willing to receive instruction and discipline, are you really that passionate about what you're pursuing?

Be open to correction. Be willing to learn. Seek out wise counsel. Be nonstop.

Think back to what you wrote on day 10. As you reflect on what you're willing to suffer for, how committed are you to the process of learning?

_____

_____

_____

_____

_____

_____

The following are various fears and barriers that hinder us in receiving instruction. Circle the ones you think most people struggle with.

Always thinking you're right	Unwillingness to learn new things
Not being open to change	Negativity
Eye rolling	Lack of self-awareness
Laziness	Disrespectfulness
Fear of rejection or failure	Arrogance
Thinking you're smarter	Ungratefulness

Which ones do you struggle with or have you struggled with in the past? Why? Circle them.

_____

_____

_____

_____

_____

As we dig into our passion, we *need* other people to guide us along the way. Do you ever ask anyone for assistance? For wisdom, guidance, knowledge? What I've learned is that people consider it an honor to help if they can!

Write the names of a couple of people you know whom you would love to learn from. In what areas of your life can they come alongside you to instruct, teach, discipline, and correct?

Name	How He or She Can Help Me Improve
1. _____	1. _____
	_____
2. _____	2. _____
	_____

Commit to the process of learning today! Be proactive and reach out to the people you listed.

The Musar Mindset

- *I will* drop my ego.
- *I will* learn from and listen to those who have more experience than I have.
- *I will* be willing to accept criticism and feedback.
- *I will* work on identified areas of improvement.
- *I will* be grateful that someone is taking time to invest in my life.
- *I will* be honest and clear in my communication.
- *I am* musar driven.

Day 13

RETHINK RISK

RISK IS RELATIVE. JUST ASK ALEX HONNOLD, THE world's best professional rock climber and free soloist. Over his lifetime, the lanky thirty-six-year-old has climbed hundreds of big rock walls all over the globe—without a rope or any safety equipment! If you've seen the award-winning *National Geographic* documentary *Free Solo*, you know that Honnold is most notably known for his free-solo ascent of Yosemite's El Capitan, a three-thousand-foot vertical wall made up of sheer granite.

The risk of free soloing is simple: If a climber falls, there is a significant chance of death. One false move, one misstep, or one mistake, and it's over. *All* over. In a 2015 interview, Honnold was asked if he thought what he did for a living was dangerous. His response was quite interesting. He said, "What I do is very high consequence, but I don't think it's particularly risky."[8]

High consequence, low risk? To you and me, that seems crazy! Hanging off a cliff a thousand feet in the air without a rope to catch my fall doesn't seem like low risk. But to Honnold, it's a shift in perspective. After spending decades training his mind and body to feel comfortable in places where most people don't, he views risk in a different light. Today I want to challenge you to do the same. I'm not asking you to free solo El Capitan, but I do believe that in our pursuit of passion, we must rethink risk.

Before we begin, how would you define the idea of risk?

_____

_____

_____

_____

In simplest terms, *risk* is when something is on the line. Risk is often thought of as the possibility of loss, injury, or danger. Whether taking a new job, investing in the stock market, or driving on the interstate (especially in Florida), risk exists. It's real, it's personal, and it's potentially painful. But risk is also perceived. Just because one person views something as risky doesn't mean it is. As Honnold demonstrated, it's about perspective.

When you begin to put everything in God's hands and live in obedience according to His Word, here is my question to you: Is that actually a risk?

_____

_____

You see, while living on this earth, you will experience some sort of suffering. That's the whole point of pursuing passion, right? As you step into your purpose, there's a chance you might lose something: relationships, finances, safety, and so on. From a human vantage point, there's risk involved in living sold out for Jesus. But when you trust God with the outcome, what do you really have to lose?

Many of us avoid putting everything on the line in pursuit of our passion because of fear—fear of failure, fear of rejection, fear of what others will think, fear of being mocked. In the prelude, we discussed how fear cripples a mission-possible life.

I've seen so many people afraid to take chances because they feared how others would perceive them. This is such a paralyzing mentality, and I've fallen victim to this just like everyone else. I'm naturally a people pleaser. But when you start to see things closer to how God does, you realize it doesn't matter what the critics say. When my dad told everyone that he was taking his wife and four kids across the ocean to be a missionary in the Philippines, was there perceived risk? Of course. There was a chance that his life wouldn't be comfortable or his family would be persecuted. People questioned and disagreed with his intentions. I'm sure all the name calling and disapproval from my dad's family and friends hurt. But he didn't hesitate going! To him, it wasn't a risk. It was what God called him to do, so it was worth everything.

When you choose God, risk is temporary and relative. Is there a risk that I could be made fun of or that someone may not like me? Sure! But that's the risk I'm willing to take. Shut out the naysayers and tune in to the voice of truth. When you take a risk for people—whom God has a heart for—to me, it's just not that much of a risk. And if it is, it's one I'm willing to take, and I hope you're willing to as well.

Spend some time assessing your own life. Think about your overall comfort level with risk. Consider what risks you are being asked to take and then write them below.

Q What risks are you taking in life, or what risks should you be taking?

A 1._____
2._____
3._____

Q What fear is associated with taking these risks?

A 1._____
2._____
3._____

Q What's on the line if you do or don't take these risks?

A 1._____
2._____
3._____

Based on what you just wrote, consider your purpose. Do these risks align with what God is calling you to do? Do you still consider them risks?

If risk is relative, how does that change the way you pursue your passion?

_____

_____

_____

_____

What if "taking a risk for God" were less about jumping off cliffs and going and more about examining our motives and opening our eyes to how God might be wanting to use us right where we are, embracing the uncomfortable in our midst?

—KRIS BECKERT,

"When Risking It All for God Means Staying Where You Are"

MODULE 3

Get Comfortable Being Uncomfortable

I don't know anyone who enjoys being uncomfortable, but I know that being uncomfortable has benefits we often don't see on the first look. Discomfort can offer you opportunities to grow and develop character, becoming better versions of yourself you never knew existed.

For the next five days, you're going to gauge your level of comfort and see the power that comes when you begin to embrace the value of discomfort.

Day 14

GET USED TO IT

IF THERE'S ONE WAY TO IMPEDE YOUR PERSONAL growth and development, keep doing the same things over and over again. Stay in the cozy corner of your comfort zone. Don't stretch beyond your perceived limitations.

According to a study conducted by Yale professor Daeyeol Lee, predictability, in a sense, shuts off your brain's learning centers. To be clear, this doesn't refer to consistency necessary to create and maintain strong habits; it's about when your routine has stopped serving you well and instead has become rote, confining, and, as a result, limiting. When that happens, consider your brain in sleep mode. Break free and try new things and—*boom!*—your mental engine begins to warm up and activate. From that place, learning and growth happens. And it's from there that your life begins to change.[1]

But this position of internal transformation and purpose begins by getting outside your comfort zone—beyond your gaming system, the cozy blanket, and endless hours of browsing on social media. It's time to get uncomfortable. Do something that doesn't come easy to you. Push yourself harder at the gym. Get up earlier in the morning. Develop your skills. Set up a meeting with your boss and ask for constructive feedback. Sign up to lead the presentation.

Auren Hoffman, entrepreneur and current CEO of SafeGraph, shares great advice for breaking through the barriers of our comfort and maximizing learning. He suggests doing hard things, the tasks that ask the most from us, 70 percent of the time.[2]

> One way people . . . underestimate themselves is by failing to spend most of their time on things that are really hard for them to do. . . . These are the tasks that result in the most growth.[3]

I may be a little aggressive in my opinion, but I think most people in Western society hate being uncomfortable. They start complaining seconds before taking a high-intensity interval-training (HIIT) class. They shirk extra responsibility because it'll rob them of quality time . . . with Netflix. They keep hitting snooze instead of getting up when the alarm sounds. They don't volunteer for anything because it'll cost them time, comfort, energy, or resources.

I don't mind being uncomfortable on mission trips because *it's a mission!* And the mission is not to be comfortable; it's to do something significant for someone else. Guess what? That means it's going to cost you. And I know that the discomfort will unlock for me the capacity to learn, grow, and adapt.

Think about a situation in which discomfort is present. Instead of wishing it away, get curious about your discomfort. How is it making you evolve?

_____

_____

_____

_____

_____

You're reading this book because you want to live a life of purpose, meaning, and significance. Get used to the fact that getting uncomfortable is part of that equation. It's going to become hard. It's going to create some anxiety. It might induce fear. You may start to doubt or second-guess yourself. Remind yourself that discomfort is a constant in a life of growth. Repeat that scenario over and over in your head. Once you accept that reality, you are going to begin to thrive in the sweet spot of productive discomfort.

You don't have to stress yourself out to the point of inducing an anxiety attack or heart attack. You just have to reach beyond the limitations you may have placed on yourself and try something new, something different, something that you know will add value and probably be challenging at the same time.

You'll never know what you are capable of unless you branch out of the predictable ordinariness of your mindset, your routine, and any habits that, if you're honest, aren't serving you in the best capacity. Keep pushing past the edge of the safe zone and embark on the adventure of what you are made of and who you were created to be.

Discomfort brings engagement and change. Discomfort means you're doing something that others were unlikely to do, because they're hiding out in the comfortable zone. When your uncomfortable actions lead to success, the organization rewards you and brings you back for more.

—SETH GODIN, *Linchpin*

Day 15

DO IT ANYWAY

MOTHER TERESA. A HOUSEHOLD NAME. A SYMBOL of compassion. A missionary nun who dedicated her life to acts of service.

Awarded the Nobel Peace Prize in 1979, Mother Teresa stands among such greats as Billy Graham, Elie Wiesel, Martin Luther King Jr., and Mahatma Gandhi, who all somehow helped shift and shape the twentieth century. Known for her Catholic faith and care for the poorest of the poor, Mother Teresa sacrificed a comfortable lifestyle to work in the slums of India, fighting for people. She learned medicine, started outdoor schools, established hospice centers, opened children's homes, distributed food to the hungry, and traveled the world, helping those in need. Her passion was to love the naked, the homeless, the orphan, the crippled, the blind, the diseased, the shunned, the unborn—all people who felt unwanted, unloved, and uncared for. Even though critics questioned her strategy and tactics, she risked her health and safety for the sake of others.

Even in her old age, Mother Teresa wasn't afraid to get uncomfortable. In August 1982, at seventy-one years old, she marched right into the thick of a bloody conflict known as the siege of Beirut. As part of the Lebanon War, Israeli planes had bombed the city of Beirut after an assassination attempt on the Israeli ambassador by Palestinian terrorist forces. This bombing raid left thirty-seven special-needs children trapped in a mental hospital in the middle of the war zone, many of whom were quite young and could not walk. They had been abandoned by the hospital staff without food, care, or hygiene. Some were dying.

A key witness recalls a polarizing conversation between Mother Teresa, a religious leader, and another man:

> Priest: "You must understand the circumstances Mother. Two weeks ago, a priest was killed. It's chaos out there. The risk is too great."
>
> Mother Teresa: "But Father . . . I believe it is our duty. We must go and take the children one by one. Risking our lives is in the order of things. All for Jesus. All for Jesus. . . ."
>
> Second man: "But do you hear the bombs?"
>
> Mother Teresa: "Yes, I hear them."[4]

The next day, despite being advised by high-ranking clergy members not to go, Mother Teresa stepped behind enemy lines. Led by prayer and conviction, she entered west Beirut and somehow negotiated a cease-fire to rescue the children. A team of Red Cross workers scooped up the left-for-dead children from the ash and debris and took them to a nearby safe home to be examined and cleaned.

Later, in a post-extraction news conference, Mother Teresa refused to discuss the politics of the Lebanese conflict, reminding journalists that the only thing that mattered was that "the children are with us."[5] Sheltered and secured, the mission was accomplished.

No matter the circumstances, Mother Teresa was willing to embrace discomfort in order to love people. If it meant driving into a war zone, she did it. If it meant speaking with terrorists, she did it. If it meant sleeping on dirt floors, she did it. If it meant going hungry so starving kids could eat, she did it. If it meant giving away money she was awarded, she did it. If it meant skipping retirement, she did it. Mother Teresa had a "do it anyway" outlook. Motivated by the beauty and value in every human being, she set the excuses aside and let her actions speak for themselves.

When pursuing a life of significance, do what you have to do to serve and influence others. Even when it's hard or people make fun, call you crazy, question your decisions, or abandon you, when fighting for people who can't fight for themselves is on the line, *do it anyway*.

As you read the conversation between Mother Teresa and the two men, what stood out to you about her response and attitude?

Keep in mind that this "do it anyway" attitude is fuel for mission living, but it can also be destructive when taken out of a healthy context: *I've already watched something I shouldn't watch, so I'll just continue to do it anyway* or *I've already had dessert, but it wouldn't hurt to eat another. I'll do it anyway.* See, I'm sure you've thought of ways you've abused this principle. What are some unhealthy habits that you need to stop "doing anyway"?

_____

_____

_____

_____

In the space below, identify two or three healthy "uncomfortable" convictions that you know you should be acting on but are not. What will the outcome be if you "do it anyway"?

I will start to . . .	When I do this . . .
1. _____	1. _____
2. _____	2. _____
3. _____	3. _____

*God's will is for us to demonstrate to a hurting world
how wonderfully His power can work within
the person who perseveres.*

—PATRICK MORLEY, *Devotions for the Man in the Mirror*

Day 16

SEE THINGS DIFFERENTLY

PERSPECTIVE IS EVERYTHING. ERIK WEIHENMAYER is one of the world's most accomplished adventure junkies, and he "sees" life a little differently. The fifty-two-year-old has kayaked the raging white waters through the Grand Canyon, skied black-diamond slopes, scaled several of the world's tallest mountains, and become a certified solo skydiver and paraglider.

So, what's special about all this? Well, besides the fact that any one of these is an incredible feat, Erik has achieved it all while being *blind*! Totally, 100 percent blind. Yes, you read that correctly.

Erik has kayaked 277 miles of the Colorado River, jumped from planes, flown paragliders, and climbed Mt. Everest . . . as a person who happens to be blind. It's remarkable. When he was four or five years old, Erik was diagnosed with an extremely rare eye disease called retinoschisis, a condition that attacks the retina. By the time he was fourteen, Erik had completely lost his vision. Feeling helpless and fearing the unknown, he struggled to adjust to his new reality. He lived in denial for some time, telling himself that he was going to get better. Eventually, he had no choice but to accept his condition. As he matured, Erik slowly learned to adapt.

In a podcast interview, he shared, "Once I accepted [blindness], my life got a lot better and then I could push the parameters of what I could do."[6]

Determined to defy the odds and live a "no barriers" life, Erik placed himself in uncomfortable situations on purpose. At the age of sixteen, he started rock climbing. Imagine how awkward and uncomfortable he must have felt the first time he got on a wall. He couldn't look up and plan out his route. He couldn't see all the different holds. All he was able to do was reach—reach as far as his hands could stretch.

By continuously taking on new levels of discomfort, Erik homed in on his other senses. He started using what others saw as pain or disability as his greatest asset. Without the distraction of sight, Erik could concentrate on the task at hand. He listened closely to the rock vibrations and could visualize the wall by grazing over the granite with his fingertips. It's fascinating how studies show that our brains respond to changes in our normal functionality by enhancing the stimulation of other senses!

In Erik's case, when he got comfortable with his new way of "seeing," it led to immeasurable achievements. Erik has now scaled all the Seven Summits, the tallest peaks on each continent, which include Denali and Kilimanjaro. He's used his discomfort as a catalyst to push him in new directions. He realized that becoming blind is just a thing that happened to him and refuses to let it be a roadblock that stops him from experiencing all that nature has to offer.

Despite his accomplishments, Erik is quick to remind people that his success didn't happen overnight. Each experience came with an immense amount of preparation *and* failure. Kayaking the Grand Canyon took six years of training. Climbing Everest took more than thirteen years. For Erik, it's not about the mountaintop view; it's about the movement, the journey that took him to the top. Let's be honest—discomfort sucks. Not many people like it. But when you realize that it takes discomfort to bust through barriers, you have to be willing to withstand it.

The more we pursue uncomfortable situations and experiences, the more we learn to see them as opportunities for growth. We don't always get to choose what adversities hit us or what obstacles are in our paths, but we do get to choose how to deal with them. The attitude, the effort, the courage—those are all choices we get to make. I think I've been most inspired by the W15H kids that our foundation has been able to serve over the past ten years. They've had to overcome so much in their lives, and they've done it with amazing attitudes. They've made the choice to see things differently—to have faith, hope, and love in the midst of their adversity. Just like Erik, those children didn't get to decide their health, but they chose a positive perspective despite the discomfort.

Most people don't think of sight as a distraction. What is something in your life that you don't perceive as being a distraction but is holding you back from focusing on mission-possible living?

How can you begin to shift your thinking into seeing that deterrent as something that can bring about positivity (for example, growth, strength in a certain area, or a new way of empathizing with others)?

_____

_____

_____

_____

We receive what we perceive.

—UNKNOWN

Day 17

PRACTICE HITTING
THE OFF-SPEED

I BELIEVE YOU GET MORE COMFORTABLE OUTSIDE your comfort zone the more you practice it.

Envision stepping into a professional batter's box, digging your back foot into the dirt, tapping the plate, and smoothly getting into your stance. Even though there are twenty-eight thousand fans screaming, eating popcorn, and buying dollar dogs, it's you versus the pitcher. Standing sixty feet, six inches away from you on the high hill, his lanky body steps onto the mound to take the sign. After shaking off his catcher twice, he finally nods his head and begins to step back in his windup. You stand there waiting for the pitch with a loose grip on your bat. Locking on his release point, *smackkk!*

Strike one! Ah, you blinked! First pitch: fastball. It went right by you at ninety-eight miles per hour, catching the outside corner of the plate. It came in a lot faster than you were expecting. Less than half a second, to be exact. It's a good thing you get three. Shake it off and get ready for the next pitch. As the pitcher receives the sign once again, you re-collect and lock back in. He winds up to deliver the 0–1 pitch. With everything you got, you swing like there's no tomorrow!

Foul ball! Strike two. You just missed it. You were on time but a tad under it. Zero and two count. Not looking good. You have a lot of ground to make up. But remember, all it takes is one pitch. Down in the count, you decide to change your approach. You're no longer looking to put one over the fence; instead, you just want to put the ball in play. You won't miss it for a third time.

Before the pitcher starts his windup, he plays around with the ball in his glove. After getting situated, he begins his motion. As he's about to throw, you shift your weight back. Here it comes. You start your swing. However, this time the ball isn't moving as fast. Unfortunately for you, the opposing team had read the scouting report. Your weakness is hitting off-speed pitches. Feeling like you're in slow motion, you lunge forward. With some serious rotation, the ball is moving right to left like your uncle doing the Electric Slide at your cousin's wedding! With your weight out on your front foot, you chase a ball in the dirt. Frozen in dismay and disgust, you give it one last pity swipe, knowing there's nothing you can do to stop your momentum.

Strike three. Why'd you swing at it? The pitcher just made you look like a T-baller swinging the bat for the first time. It was a nasty curveball, one of the toughest pitches to hit. Not only does it throw you off your timing, but also you never know when it's coming. All you can do is better prepare for it next time.

Here's the point: Life's not always a meaty fastball right down the middle. It's full of off-speed pitches. Curveballs. Changeups. Sliders. Knuckleballs. They take the form of a broken bone, a busted radiator, an unexpected market crash, and a worldwide pandemic. There's plenty of unforeseen circumstances that are totally out of your control that produce discomfort.

Do you ever practice hitting life's curveballs? Do you take the time to put yourself in uncomfortable situations, so that when the time comes, you're able to adapt?

The more you practice being uncomfortable, the more comfortable you are in times of discomfort. I remember my first time stepping up to the plate after not playing organized baseball for twelve years. The curveball at the professional level was extremely difficult to hit. It was very uncomfortable. But in order to get better, I had to practice—and then practice some more. Though I didn't master the curveball, I had gotten a lot more comfortable at the plate by the time I retired from baseball.

This is simple psychology. The more you practice something, the better you get. As we've discussed, comfort produces complacency, and complacency hinders mission-possible living. Don't let discomfort prevent you from maximizing your God-given ability.

As you know, baseball is a reaction game. Unless you're the pitcher, there's not a whole lot you can control. Life is similar. Uncertainty is inevitable, but we can train our minds and bodies to be ready to react.

What's your attitude toward discomfort?

_____

_____

_____

_____

Identify one or two ways you can start practicing being uncomfortable. Maybe it's starting that new online training course or beginning each day with a cold shower. It can even be as simple as texting a friend whom you haven't talked to in a while or having that tough conversation with your spouse. Remember, the more you practice, the better you get at something.

1. _____

2. _____

*I am convinced that life is 10% what happens to me
and 90% of how I react to it.*
—CHARLES R. SWINDOLL

Day 18

FIGHT THE FUNK

IN *MISSION POSSIBLE,* I TELL THE STORY OF TRAVEL-ing to Texas for a speaking event at the Omni Hotel in the Dallas Fort Worth metropolitan area. I didn't realize at the time that I'd be staying and speaking at the corporate headquarters and entertainment complex of the Dallas Cowboys. I was given a tour of the Cowboys' incredible facilities, including the state-of-the-art twelve-thousand-seat indoor arena that houses the Texan NFL team as well as acts as a stadium for eight high school teams, a football-shaped locker room, and an all-digital war room.

Later that night, I'd be sharing words of encouragement to a couple hundred people. I was psyched about that. I really was. At the same time, I noticed my spirit dip a little further into unpleasant feelings and thoughts as I toured the facilities. Where I was in that moment reminded me of where I wasn't in my life.

Seeing the Cowboys' facilities made me miss football. The disappointment dug itself deeper into my spirit, and I found myself thinking these things:

I wish I had the chance to be part of this facility.
I wish I had what they had.
I wish I would have . . .
I wish I did . . .
God, I wish You had a different plan.

I'm almost embarrassed to admit this, but I stayed in that sphere of funk until I walked onto the stage hours later and began to share my heart and words of encouragement with a group of people. And when that happened, in an instant my joy was complete. I wasn't thinking of the grandiosity of the Cowboys' facilities or wishing I were on an NFL roster; I was enjoying and using the gifts God gave me to share with others words of hope, faith, and love. I'm not saying those feelings and thoughts are gone forever. They still pop up uninvited and unannounced every now and then. But I try my best to fight that funk by doing something for someone else.

I'm sure you've heard of a runner's high. It's when you are engaging in intense cardiovascular exercise (such as running) and a flood of endorphins, the body's natural happy chemicals, are released, thereby overwhelming you with pure elation, less stress, and a reduced state of pain and discomfort. You may have even experienced this phenomenon yourself. It's pretty cool, right? I bet you haven't heard of this less common term: *the helper's high.*

The helper's high was coined in the late 1980s,[7] when reports surfaced confirming that positive emotions followed selfless service to others. Studies kept coming. Research in neuroscience and psychology supports the theory that helping others brings happiness your way.

When we feel depressed, lonely, sad, or disappointed, our impulse is to wallow in those feelings. But when we shift our focus onto others and selflessly do something for someone else, our own spirits get lifted in the process. This feeds our soul. I'm not saying that donating money, sending an encouraging note, or helping a stranger carry groceries is going to forever eliminate all negative feelings that show up in your mind, soul, and spirit. But when those negative feelings arrive, help another person. Get out of your head and do something nice for someone else.

Whenever I'd feel low or face unexpected criticism, I would find myself feeling edgy and depressed. To battle those cumbersome feelings, I would ask a good friend of mine to accompany me on a visit to a local hospital to visit sick kids. We'd spend time with amazing people who struggled to overcome challenges I couldn't even fathom. It's amazing what happens when you intentionally fight your way out of a funk. It puts your own life in perspective. It fosters a spirit of gratitude. It pushes you outside your bubble and into the dynamic tapestry of humanity. It increases positivity. Truly, it's a beautiful thing.

The next time you find yourself in a bad mood, look outward. Who can you help? Who can you serve? Who can you encourage? Go out of your way to create opportunities for this to happen. Altruism always pays dividends—not just for others, but for your own well-being.

In the space below, write about a time when you made someone feel special. What did you do? Why did you do it? How did it make the other person feel? What was his or her response? What emotions were stirring within you?

_____

_____

_____

_____

_____

As you recall this account, I hope you find joy and contentment!

Do all the good you can, by all the means you can, in all the ways you can, in all the places you can, at all the times you can, to all the people you can, as long as ever you can.
—JOHN WESLEY, *Letters of John Wesley*

MODULE 4

Get Locked In

Many of us struggle with wandering minds and the ability to stay focused. Imagine how much you could accomplish if you kept yourself from getting distracted every five minutes. Living mission possible to your fullest potential is hindered if you can't harness your ability to show up, focus, and finish what you start. My hope is that if this is something you battle with, the next five days will give you solid footing to help you get and stay in the zone.

Day 19

MASTER YOUR ATTENTION

ANGELA DUCKWORTH, AUTHOR OF *GRIT: THE POWER of Passion and Perseverance*, said, "Some would argue that human attention, not money, is the most valuable commodity there is. It's the ultimate scarce resource."[1] I believe that's a true statement. In 2000, the average human attention span was around twelve seconds. In a study Microsoft conducted in 2015, that number dropped to eight. To put this in perspective, a goldfish can hold its attention for about nine seconds.[2]

We can thank our hyperdigitized environment for that shocking number. From the addictive nature of social media, smartphones, and information overload, we have a hard time staying on task. Whether we're completing a proposal, organizing a fundraiser, or drawing up a marketing plan, there are always hidden voices competing for our attention. Scroll through these pics. Buy those jeans. Google what's trending on Twitter. Keep a constant pulse on the news cycle so you don't miss out on anything. And our lack of attention has serious consequences: our ability to focus can mean the difference between success and failure.

Our waning level of attention is not tied to just technology; it has become our state of mind. According to a Harvard study, the average person's mind wanders 47 percent of the time during most of their activities.[3] Our minds wander when we exercise, work, commute, engage in conversations, and do housework. You probably have a pretty good gauge of what your general level of focus is during any given activity. If you're unsure, use the following scale to rate your current attention level.

Circle your score.

Really struggling to concentrate   No problem focusing on
                                                            the task at hand

1   2   3   4   5   6   7   8   9   10

If You Circled 1–3

You are likely the owner of many unfinished tasks. You are probably an avid daydreamer. In fact, right now you might be thinking about where you're going to dinner instead of finishing reading this sentence. Experts suggest that our minds wander for as much as 50 percent of our waking moments! To keep your mind from straying, it's time to focus on mastering your attention.[4] Look into attention-taming resources or even the help of a professional to get your mind on track and your life in control.

If You Circled 4–6

You may find it easier to focus on things you enjoy doing, watching, listening to, or learning about. Don't we all! You may have a hard time paying attention to details and find it doesn't take but a few minutes for you to start thinking about anything other than what you need to be focusing on at the moment. Consider less time multitasking and more time single-tasking. The brain doesn't do the best job handling a hundred things at once. Give it a rest sometimes. Try mono-tasking. If you haven't already, think about maintaining a planner or goal calendar. (This book is a great start!) Write stuff down and start prioritizing and organizing to free up space!

If You Circled 7–9

You are consciously aware of how you spend your attention. You don't avoid or resist projects that require sustained mental efforts. You recognize when your mind starts to drift and are able to redirect your attention to what you're supposed to do. If there's one thing I can say about improving your attention performance, it is to monitor your social media usage. I know, you've heard it before, right? But it's a huge culprit in sucking the attention out of us. Just keep an eye on it, that's all. Ask yourself, *Who is earning my attention?*

If You Circled 10

Well, you are superhuman. Share the love with others so we can have more attention masters out there!

* * *

Whether we're fantasizing about that dream vacation during the board meeting or getting sucked into the vortex of social media while we're supposed to be researching a paper, we seem to be losing a lot more than we are gaining. Most of all, we are losing time, something none of us can afford to waste. A study from the University of California, Irvine, shows that although distractions are common in the workplace and most of the interrupted work gets resumed the same day, a transition takes places between the distraction and resumed work. It takes an average of twenty-three minutes to get back to the task.[5] Small interruptions during the day can add up to a lot of lost time.

If we want to grow, live better, and make our lives count, we have to harness our ability to concentrate. Mastering attention is a lot like mastering the physical body. The more you work at it, the stronger it gets.

Some distractions are unavoidable. If your child just puked his or her breakfast, your day is going to be interrupted. If your boss is asking for urgent information that will affect the merger taking place in two hours, whatever else you're working on likely will have to wait. And if you just got engaged, yes, I expect you to be daydreaming about your wedding. That said, the key is to limit the distractions as much as possible. Pay attention to your attention.

Here are some suggestions.

Hack your personal space. If this is possible, create a quiet atmosphere with minimal distractions. Get off your phone as much as you can. I know it's hard, but it'll be okay. I promise. At the very least, turn off the notifications so your background noise isn't a cacophony of dings letting you know someone just posted another selfie or that your kicks are on sale.

Try the Pomodoro Technique. This is a time-management method that helps you fight distractions and trains your brain at the same time. It's also simple. If you're doing a large task and struggling to maintain consistent attention, break it down into smaller chunks of time. Start by setting a timer for twenty-five (or forty-five or sixty) minutes. During that entire period of time, work. Don't check your email. Don't google anything. Don't grab coffee or rummage for a snack. Work. When the time is over, take a few minutes to do whatever you want, and then get back to the timer and start again.

Stay present. Mindfulness is so important. Being aware of where you are and with whom will help you stay in the moment and can tame mind wandering. When you start daydreaming or wondering what the name of that actor is from the movie you saw in the sixth grade, tighten the reins on your brain and redirect your focus to what's happening in the present.

List the things that distract you the most.

_____

_____

_____

_____

How can you set limits or guardrails to prevent these distractions?

_____

_____

_____

_____

Our addictive, digitized environment will not stop bombarding us with information anytime soon, but that doesn't mean it gets to boss us around. Starting today, master your attention by being aware of and taming the chaos and the noise. When your focus is balanced and healthy, you're going to find the time and peace of mind to make your life count.

> *If you don't pay appropriate attention to what has your attention, it will take more of your attention than it deserves.*
> —DAVID ALLEN, *Making It All Work*

Day 20

CREATE A
SENSE OF URGENCY

MOST OF THE PEOPLE I ADMIRE WHO HAVE ACCOM-
plished great feats have a few things in common. One of them is a
healthy sense of urgency. I think of my dad and again of Demi-Leigh, in
particular. Whether it's my dad trying to preach to every single person
in the Philippines, or Demi-Leigh leaving no stone unturned in her desire to grow and learn to get to the next level, they understand the importance of doing now what will lead them forward in their purposes.
And they are willing to accept the cost.

Before we get to what a sense of urgency is, here's what it isn't. It's
NOT an emergency or an after-the-fact response to a crisis. If we treat
all of life as an emergency, we will run out of energy and leave little
room for creativity and growth. Being spun in a cyclone of an emergency quashes the desire to make a difference in the lives of others. A
healthy sense of urgency is nothing like this. There's always going to be
a reactionary element to life, but we can develop a sense of urgency that
is proactive, not reactive.

John Kotter, Harvard Business School professor and author of the bestselling book *A Sense of Urgency,* states that urgency is a necessary ingredient in the recipe of a successful organization, particularly when it comes to implementing change. In its absence, most people won't feel the push to work a little harder. But Kotter explains that urgency is a marathon, not a sprint: "With an attitude of true urgency, you try to accomplish something important each day, never leaving yourself with a heart-attack-producing task of running one thousand miles in the last week of the race."[6]

You Have a Sense of Urgency If You . . .

- **respect time and have an appropriate deadline for tasks.**
- **are proactive, not reactive.**
- **act with clarity and purpose.**
- **have an intense desire to execute, not a frenetic state of being busy.**
- **compel your thoughts into action.**
- **feel an internal sense of responsibility.**

Complacency is the enemy of urgency. It's also one of the biggest opponents of living a mission-possible life, because complacency breeds stagnation. We're most susceptible to this threat when we think that what we've got is good enough. That there is no need for change, development, or growth. That the status quo isn't terrible, so why the push for better or more?

As a believer, you are God's masterpiece. But that doesn't mean you are a finished product. Instead, in your partnership with the Creator of the universe, you get to fulfill your part in pushing a mission forward.

And you can't bring hope to a dark world when you're steeped in complacency. When you live with a sense of urgency, you are aware of needed change and are ready and willing to act.

Read on for a few ways to foster a sense of urgency.

1. **Create tangible goals and a hard deadline—and meet them.** If you're overwhelmed by so much to do, stop indulging a cycle of procrastination. Instead, set small but concrete goals. Then you can knock them out, one by one.

2. **Be aware of signs of complacency.** Catch yourself when you start getting lazy, and do one thing to back out of that comfort zone. For instance, if you find yourself disengaged from what you're supposed to do, get back in the game by reading a book, listening to a podcast, watching a documentary, or meeting with someone with experience on the topic to fire up your engagement.

3. **Stay disciplined.** Figure out what distractions and obstacles most often stand in your way, and where possible, block them out. Stop checking email. Take a break from social media. Set a timer for blocks of uninterrupted, focused work.

4. **Leverage anxiety into action.** Instead of allowing frenetic energy to paralyze you from doing anything, use it as fuel to do one thing—just one. And once you've done that, do the next thing, and the one after that, one task at a time.

Start Now

1. Do you struggle with procrastination in one area more than in another? Why do you think that is?

_____

_____

_____

_____

_____

2. Think about a big task you've been putting off. Do it today. Don't just make a plan for when you'll have time for it. Write out some steps you can take today to move forward and then start doing them now. (After you put this book down, of course.)

_____

_____

_____

_____

_____

Time passes, and it never needs our permission. Don't wait until you have no choice but to take action. If there is something aligned with a mission-possible life that demands your attention, do it now. Don't wait. Turn "someday" into "today."

Progressive improvement beats delayed perfection.
—MARK TWAIN

Day 21

CULTIVATE CONSISTENCY

YOU CAN'T GO TO THE DENTIST ONCE AND THEN expect your teeth to stay clean. You must brush twice a day for two minutes, plus floss each time you brush. In the same vein, you can't expect to work out once a month and be in optimal shape. You have to exercise far more regularly over a longer period of time before you will see progress.

I don't know anyone who has accomplished a life of significance who did so overnight. Why is Tom Brady the GOAT? Because he's been to ten Super Bowls. And how was he able to get to ten Super Bowls? One word: consistency.

The dictionary defines the word *consistency* as "steadfast adherence to the same principles, course, form, etc."[7] I believe consistency comes from the will to make the same choices over and over and over again. We can live mission possible and make our lives count when we consistently make the hard and uncomfortable choices in order to pursue purpose.

I've heard people attribute an athlete's success to his or her drive, saying, "Oh, so-and-so has such a will to win." I think that's ridiculous. Everyone has the will to win. In all my years on the field, I've never played with anyone who didn't want to win that game, but some of them had more of a will to prepare six months before the season started. Successful athletes have the will to prepare and practice. They consistently train harder than their competitors.

What Consistency Does

- **develops discipline and self-control**
- **establishes a track record**
- **fast-tracks improvement**
- **creates personal responsibility**
- **makes an individual dependable and trustworthy**

Consistency isn't about perfection. Setbacks happen. Hiccups—whether getting sick, taking care of people who get sick, unforeseen pandemics that throw everything off course, or unexpected life events—interrupt the best of schedules. If we're temporarily knocked off the rail and can't maintain consistency, we simply do our best and prepare for the sequel. Setbacks don't mean we'll never get to play again.

You illustrate consistency when your heart wants to make the right choice, your will chooses the discipline, and you put forth focused action to get it done.

Heart + Will + Focused Action = Consistency

Say you have a bad habit of being late everywhere you go. Your heart might be in the right place of wanting to be punctual, but if you don't check your phone and monitor your progress and time, you will continue to be late.

Without consistency, it will be nearly impossible to take the steps to make your life count. Think about something you want to accomplish. Identify one task you need to do to make it happen. Track that task in an app or separate journal for thirty days and note your progress. Make appropriate adjustments and keep at it for another thirty days until the task becomes a habit.

What is that task?

_____

_____

_____

_____

Beginning to cultivate consistency in your life may look like repetition at first. That's okay. Over time, it evolves into a habit. And eventually it becomes second nature and produces the desired outcome.

Don't rush the process. Consistency doesn't develop quickly. It happens gradually, one step, one choice, repeated over and over again.

> *Changes that seem small and unimportant at first*
> *will compound into remarkable results if you're willing*
> *to stick with them for years.*
> —JAMES CLEAR, *Atomic Habits*

Day 22

LISTEN TO THE RIGHT VOICE

I'M CONFIDENT YOU KNOW THAT YOUR FINGER-
prints are unique. No one else in the world has the exact same pattern of
ridges, swirls, and lines that exists on your fingers. Even identical twins,
who share the same DNA, have different fingerprints. But did you know
that your voice is just as unique to you as your fingerprints are? You may
sound like your sibling, and your aunt may have trouble recognizing
you over the telephone, but no two voices are exactly alike.

Different parts of the body are involved in creating the voice that's
unique to you, from the length and tension of your vocal cords to the
shape and size of your mouth, nose, and throat, which help produce the
actual human sound. We can recognize many things from the sound of
a voice alone. Imagine sitting in front of someone on an airplane and
listening to him or her talk. Just by listening to the voice, you can likely
gather many details about the person, such as gender, size, age, and
mood and maybe even what part of the world he or she is from.

As unique as the human voice is to its owner, earwitness testimony is
not always reliable. If there is more than one voice talking at the same

time, distinguishing one voice from another is complicated. The hub-bub of noise vying for one's attention can be deafening. Unless we are consciously listening to one sound in particular, most of what we hear is indistinguishable noise. And it may get so loud and overwhelming that we'd much rather tune it all out.

This reminds me of when I played football for the University of Florida. Several hours before every home game, the team and I would climb into the buses parked in front of our hotel, ride right by the stadium, and stop at the Gator Walk on University Avenue. Thousands of Gator fans formed a tunnel that led to a brick sidewalk into the north end of the stadium. I was the first to get off the bus and enter the screaming crowd of fans and alumni. As a chorus of decibel-threatening cheers exploded from the wait-ing throng, accompanied by adrenaline-fueled Gator chomps, I'd wait by the curb to hug all my teammates as they stepped out from the buses. And as I'd take my first steps down that path into the stadium, I'd turn up one of my favorite songs, Casting Crowns' "Voice of Truth."

It's not that I didn't appreciate the supercharged energy of the crowd through their shouts and whistles and high fives and chomps. Of course I did. But the song was a strategy. I couldn't allow myself to get over-whelmed by the other voices around me.

One of the first voices was pride. *They're here for you, Timmy. This is pretty cool!* Then another voice: judgment. *But if they saw you on your worst day, they probably wouldn't like you.* And more voices:

You're not enough.

You can't handle the pressure.

You don't deserve to be here.

As the clamor of voices demanded my attention, I'd have to force my-self to remember the voice of Truth and whose I am and that He has a plan and purpose for my life.

What voices call out to you as you to try to live a life of purpose? Do they rehash past mistakes? Dredge up insecurities? Compare you to a teammate or colleague and announce how far you fall short? In these moments, instead of letting the negative voices try to discredit the evidence that you are unique, one of one, wonderfully and purposefully made, listen to the voice of Truth. Listen to what the Creator says about you.

God has a plan for your life.

You are here for a reason.

You can make a difference in the lives of others.

You have what it takes to fulfill what you are supposed to do.

You are loved.

Just as your audible fingerprint is unique to you, God's voice will always be the one encouraging you, rooting for you, and cheering you on. And if you listen closely enough, you'll learn to recognize His voice above all others—that "still small voice" (1 Kings 19:12, NKJV) inside your heart. It's not loud or overbearing; it's quiet. He is speaking. And His voice is the one that will shape your life with purpose.

Tomorrow we will begin exploring the idea of rest and recovery. To prepare, there will be no exercises today. Enjoy the day off. Can't wait to talk about recovery!

> *These voices—the inner critic, the inner nag, the inner pest, the inner jerk, and all the other monsters who try to talk you out of moving forward—are the part of you that is threatened by change and progress. We all have them. They are trying to protect you from new and scary things, but they are out of sync with you right now and not helpful. They hate what you are doing, but that doesn't make them right.*
>
> —DANNY GREGORY, *Art Before Breakfast*

Day 23

DON'T FORGET TO REFUEL

THE FAMOUS TOUR DE FRANCE IS ONE OF THE
largest annual sporting events in the world. Each year, roughly twelve
million spectators show up to watch 198 cyclists race across 3,500 kilometers of French terrain over a period of 21 days.[8] For professional bike
riders, this is considered the Super Bowl of cycling!

Teams strenuously compete for pride, prestige, and prize money. Av-
eraging 225 kilometers per day, riders race over various elevations (hills,
mountains, country roads, city streets), climbing from sea level to 2,000
meters, sometimes multiple times a day. It is a grueling event that takes
an enormous amount of focus and preparation.

The Tour is one of the most demanding endurance competitions in
sports history. It requires cyclists to overcome severe mental and physical fatigue. I can only imagine how sore their legs are after each day!
With one goal in mind, the bikers push their bodily limits in pursuit of
the finish line. This is not a race for the faint of heart, but to them, the
reward is worth the strain.

In a similar way, living mission possible is not a cakewalk. It requires hard work and sacrifice. Over the past several weeks, we've been digging into the reality of mission living. It takes practice, discipline, faith, and effort. It might not always seem fun or be comfortable, but it's in the pain where we learn and grow the most.

In order to live with purpose, meaning, and significance, we must be able to lock in and answer the call at any time. Every moment matters. However, as we all know, we cannot go nonstop for 24 hours, 365 days a year. Even the cyclists in the Tour de France have rest days! Two, to be exact—one between stages nine and ten, and the other between stages fifteen and sixteen. These athletes understand that in order to perform at the highest level, they must refuel and recover. I think there are several valuable lessons here.

1. Rest Is Vital

We live in a culture that takes pride in the grind. And trust me—I'm all about the grind. But we can get so caught up in the grind, a.k.a. the busyness of life, that we forget to stop. Without a doubt, rest and rejuvenation is incredibly important. If you do not take time to refuel your mind, body, and spirit, all aspects of your life—relationships, family time, physical and mental health, your job—will suffer. To keep accelerating in life's race, you must learn to rest well.

2. Rest Comes After Work

On the flip side, it's probably not wise to rest more than you actually work. These cyclists in the Tour push themselves. They get out there and go after it! Each recovery day is for the purpose of refueling their bodies so they can get back out on the roads and maximize their energy. I caution you not to err on the side of "Rest more, work less." So, you enter heaven a little bit more rested? No, I want to enter heaven with a lot more effect and impact! Living mission possible starts with the work. The rest comes after.

3. Rest Is Intentional

Recovery doesn't equate to laziness. Often people think of taking a break as an opportunity to sit on the couch and watch Netflix all day. Rest doesn't mean to abandon all forms of discipline in our lives. Structure is still needed or we can get lost in complacency. Take a look at the Great Britain Cycling Team's rest-day schedule during the Tour de France.[9] It is still planned out with plenty of time allotted for recovery.

British Cycling Team Rest-Day Schedule
• **9:30 a.m.–10:00 a.m.—Riders permitted to sleep in**
• **10:00 a.m.—Breakfast**
• **11:00 a.m.—Light ride lasting around two hours**
• **1:00 p.m.—Lunch and massage**
• **3:00 p.m.—Afternoon nap**
• **4:00 p.m.—Team brief**
• **6:30 p.m.—Dinner followed by an early night**

When we rest, we use it to rejuvenate. When did you last take time to rest and refuel? What did that look like?

_____

_____

_____

_____

_____

What are healthy ways you find rest and rejuvenation?

_____

_____

_____

_____

_____

To be intentional in planning out what your next rest days will look like, fill in the blanks below and commit to the changes you want to make.

Rest Date	Recovery Plan
_____	I will wake up at _____.
_____	In the morning, I will _____.
_____	In the afternoon, I will _____.
_____	In the evening, I will _____.
_____	I will go to bed at _____.
_____	I will wake up at _____.
_____	In the morning, I will _____.
_____	In the afternoon, I will _____.
_____	In the evening, I will _____.
_____	I will go to bed at _____.
_____	I will wake up at _____.
_____	In the morning, I will _____.
_____	In the afternoon, I will _____.
_____	In the evening, I will _____.
_____	I will go to bed at _____.

Come to Me, all who are weary and burdened,
and I will give you rest.
—MATTHEW 11:28

MODULE 5

Strain and Strive

There is no mission-possible life without effort—without putting in the work and doing your best. Straining and striving isn't the formula for achieving perfection, nor is it a money-back guarantee that all your goals will be accomplished. But it is part of the hustle you're going to need to run the race that is set before you. The next five days will help you see what that can look like.

Day 24

SEEKING SUCCESS?
ASK TWO QUESTIONS

BECOMING AN ENTREPRENEUR, GROWING YOUR business, or just excelling in your occupation—these successes are essential to achieving a better future for you and those around you.

But success comes in many ways. It doesn't come with just money or fame. We must always remember what we are straining and striving for. True success comes from doing something we love and loving and serving others while we do it. Not only is that a picture of success, but it's also what it means to live lives of significance.

When we succeed in material ways, we get to move up, take vacations, and see the fruits of our efforts. But when we strive for eternal significance, we become compelled to share and give back. When we succeed, we affect our own lives. When we are significant, we affect the lives of others. To transcend from individual success to lasting significance, we have to take our gifts, find needs, and meet them. Achieving significance means going beyond gaining financial or other comfort and striving to serve others.

To be truly successful, aim for significance. And to achieve significance, ask yourself these two questions:

1. *What am I known for?*

2. *Why not today?*

Let's break them down.

What am I known for? This question will dig into your character. Here are more questions that will help you answer that one. What do people say about you when you are not in the room? What kind of feedback do you receive from your friends, spouse, boss, coworkers, or mentor? What do your trusted friends think of you? In the space below, write down what comes to mind. If you hesitate to jot down words or phrases that seem negative, don't. They may warrant a second look. Maybe a little scrutiny can help you learn something about yourself that you never wanted to admit.

_____

_____

_____

_____

Take a look at what you wrote. Circle the words or phrases that make you cringe a little, the ones about your character that you'd like to change. Maybe you're often late to meetings or have a tendency to exaggerate the truth. Write those things down in the space below. Reflect on what you need to do, starting today, to change that behavior. Perhaps it's as simple as reading a book to learn how to shift a negative habit into a positive one. Maybe you should seek a licensed counselor or therapist to figure out the root of your behavior or unhealthy patterns. Focus on one or two habits and write an action plan of three steps you will take to make a change.

_____

_____

_____

_____

I encourage you to do this self-awareness exercise once a month. It's another way to view your strengths and weaknesses and remind yourself of certain areas that may need work so you can be who you want to be.

This question about what you are known for is challenging, but if you want to live a life of significance, it's an important question to ask. Strive over time to answer that question with qualities that make a lasting difference, such as faith, hope, and love.

Why not today? This is one of my favorite questions. In fact, I wrote a book titled *This Is the Day,* which is all about not putting off until tomorrow what God is calling you to do today, whether overcoming a bad habit, fighting for what's right, or chasing after that dream.

Reflect on the past six months to a year (or more). What are two things that you have been wanting to do or change but have been putting off? Write it on the next page.

_____

_____

_____

_____

Now list the reason behind the procrastination.

_____

_____

_____

_____

Paint a word picture of what it could look like if you accomplished what you have been putting off. How would that add value to your life? To the lives of others?

_____

_____

_____

_____

What can you do, starting today, to move forward and begin to tackle these items?

_____

_____

_____

_____

When is the best time to pursue your passion? Today. When is the best time to make a difference? Today. When is the best time to do something different? Today. When is the best time to change a life (yours or someone else's) for the better? Today. Why not today? Each day that we are given on this earth is a gift. Each day may not run as smoothly as we would like, but it's always an opportunity to grow, learn, serve, teach, and love. Going for it, even when the going is tough, is the only way to play. And this means doing what it takes every day, not just in the seasons when others are watching or something is at stake. It's important to be and do our best and strive for significance on an ordinary Tuesday.

What are you waiting for?

A life is not important
except in the impact it has on other lives.
—JACKIE ROBINSON

Day 25

AIM FOR
MORE THAN AVERAGE

IN DR. ATUL GAWANDE'S BESTSELLING BOOK
Better: A Surgeon's Notes on Performance, he investigates the world of medical professionals and what it looks like when they go from good to great. He examines the bell curve that exists among physicians—the wide gap between the best and the worst. Dr. Gawande posits that most doctors exist in the middle, the space of mediocrity. He challenges them to improve their performance and strive to become positive deviants on that curve. In an interview with the *New Yorker,* he said this:

When you plot out the bell curve for physicians, you realize very quickly that half of us must be below average, and that a good ninety per cent of us are not really at the top, after all. . . . It's hard for most of us to admit to ourselves that we're pretty middling, or even mediocre. It goes against the grain of what we're promising to people, and it also goes against our idea of ourselves.[1]

I have a feeling that Dr. Gawande's observation applies to more professions than just medicine. How many of us live our lives numbly maneuvering through the motions, giving the bare minimum? Life seems empty and uneventful. You find yourself with more free time than goals and dreams. Nothing out of the ordinary happens. Time ticks by with more of the same—more social media scrolling and binge-watching.

I don't believe that God calls us to be average. He didn't design us that way. You are one of one, created in love, by Love and for love. You are a masterpiece who has a purpose. You are made for more than just getting by.

Think of ways you have settled. Maybe you were offered a higher position but turned it down because you were afraid you wouldn't be able to handle the pressure. Perhaps you always wanted to write a book but never got past the first few pages. Journal about that experience.

How has settling for mediocrity created setbacks or limitations in your life?

_____

_____

_____

_____

_____

What happens to you as a person when you do something above what's merely required?

_____

_____

_____

_____

How to Avoid Average Clue Card

- **Don't plan your life on the opinions of others.**
- **Get comfortable with getting uncomfortable.**
- **Take responsibility.**
- **Dream big.**
- **Always access your purpose.**
- **Elevate convictions over feelings.**
- **Do what no one else is willing to do.**

I don't think anyone tries to be average. He or she just settles into that comfortable space for such reasons as fear, limiting beliefs, and lack of confidence—some of the things I addressed in the first few chapters of this book.

Don't allow the adversary of average—mediocrity—to rob you of your purpose. If you notice that progression in certain areas of your life has stalled, stop. Now that you've paused, rethink your priorities. Re-evaluate your commitment to those things, and reroute your energies into executing them.

Rising above average will not happen by accident. It takes intention. On your climb above average, you may fail. You may need to take some detours. Sometimes you realize there are people around you impeding your growth. The choice to become a positive deviant on the bell curve is yours. It's up to you. I would rather be an outlier and fail but at least try. When you're an outlier, when you don't do what everybody else is doing, you have a chance to be special. You get to experience the masterpiece you really are!

Don't just hope for more. Live for more.
—TIM TEBOW

Day 26

FIND YOUR EDGE

PRIOR TO THE SUMMER OF 1954, RUNNING A SUB-four-minute mile was considered humanly impossible. It was on the same level of athletic achievement as climbing Mt. Everest. Though a few runners had gotten close during the war years, it was thought to be an unbreakable barrier, and even a potentially dangerous pursuit.

However, on the morning of May 6 that year, crowds gathered to watch Englishman Roger Bannister, a twenty-five-year-old Oxford University medical student, attempt what no one had ever done.

Bannister, regarded as Britain's best middle-distance runner at the time, had been expected to retire from running two years prior, after the 1952 Olympics in Helsinki, Finland. But when he finished fourth in the men's 1500-meter, he knew he couldn't end his career on such a disappointing note.

He decided to set a new goal for himself: become the first person to run a mile in less than four minutes.

I wonder what was going through his head as he stepped up to the starting line that morning. Nerves? Questions? Possible doubts? Intense focus? It doesn't matter. When the starting pistol went off and he exploded forward on the track, all unnecessary emotions were left behind.

For the first two laps, Bannister paced himself behind his teammate Chris Brasher. After reaching the halfway mark in one minute fifty-eight seconds, he picked up speed and closely followed behind his other teammate, Christopher Chataway. As he rounded lap three and began his fourth and final lap, the crowd's roar grew louder. Bannister was on pace, but in order to break the world record, he was going to have to finish his last lap in under fifty-nine seconds. As he lengthened his stride and sped past Chataway, he gave it his all in his final push toward the finish line.

On the brink of collapsing, Bannister lunged forward, completing the race, and fell into the arms of a nearby spectator. Over the crackling PA system, the announcer declared the champion's official time: "3:59:04."[2]

History had been made.

In recalling his achievement, Bannister explained, "Doctors and scientists said that breaking the four-minute mile was impossible, that one would die in the attempt. Thus, when I got up from the track after collapsing at the finish line, I figured I was dead."[3]

For Bannister, and other runners at that time, running a sub-four is what I call their "edge."

Typically, when you the hear the word *edge* in sports, you think of what gives you a leg up on your competition. It's that motivating factor or secret trump card you've been holding on to. But I want to challenge you to think of the edge in a different way. I want to you think of it as a barrier: not necessarily the edge of a cliff, but a wall that hinders you from becoming your most elite.

The edge is that point of discomfort where you tend to stop—a point where life challenges you to get better. It is a barrier that requires you to stretch, push, and move past your comfort zone.

Bannister's edge was not being able to run a mile in less than four minutes. His closest recorded time prior to May 6 was a 4:02.[4] At that point, he had reached his physical limit. But just because no one had done it didn't mean it was impossible. It took mental and physical strain to step out of his comfort zone, train harder, and bust through that barrier.

The edge is that box that you don't want to step outside of or that line you don't want to cross because it's hard. It's what is standing in your way between who you are now and who you want to become.

There are edges in marriage, in school, in sports, in the workplace—all over your life. The edge either forces you to get better or keeps you in a spot of complacency.

To get a breakthrough at the edge, you must choose to do whatever it takes. What I love about the concept of the edge is that it's a key personal decision point on your journey. If you've reached the end of your natural talent or if growth has come to a standstill, you can choose discomfort and sacrifice to get better. The edge calls for serious self-reflection and a desire to change.

Most people refuse to find their edges. Why? Because they don't want to come close to pain, vulnerability, or failure. The edge shuts people down. One of the worst things you can do is stay where you are. Maybe you'll never reach your maximum God-given ability, but you can at least try!

The next time you are confronted with a barrier, begin to think through some of these questions:

- *What's the worst thing that can happen if I try and fail?*
- *What's the best thing that can happen?*
- *What am I really afraid of?*
- *Why am I doing this?*
- *What's the real goal that I have?*

What edges have you encountered in your life, and how did you overcome them?

Edge/Barrier	How I Overcame It
1. _____	1. _____
2. _____	2. _____
3. _____	3. _____

Now let's take inventory of your current reality.

Q What goals do you want to accomplish in the future?

A _____
_____

Q What are the potential edges that could keep you from accomplishing your goals?

A _____
_____

Q What will it cost you to break through these barriers?

A _____

_____

The man who can drive himself further once the effort gets painful is the man who will win.

—SIR ROGER BANNISTER

Day 27

REFRAME FAILURE

WHEN I DECIDED TO GO AFTER THE DREAM OF PLAYing professional baseball, those closest to me supported my decision. From other people, I heard some less-than-positive responses.

There were the carefully worded comments from those I knew questioned my passionate redirection but didn't want to kill my enthusiasm. "Are you sure about this?" "Have you thought about how hard it could be?" Then there were the direct hits, which I appreciated for the mere fact that they weren't soaked in sugar. "It's bad for your brand." "You're too old." "It might work, but only if you do it with a reality TV show."

In the headlines and the general public's chatter, most of the responses I got were unfavorable: "Who does he think he is?" "This is just a publicity stunt." I'm used to hearing critics, usually behind screens, so I wasn't surprised. But I'll never forget the interview I did with a friend of mine, Stephen A. Smith at *First Take*. Questioning my transition from one sport to another, Smith told me that since my "chances of success seem to be greater in football rather than baseball,"[5] why would I switch to a sport in which I was so inexperienced? He was asking, in other words, "Why try if you'll probably fail?"

His question got me so fired up. I explained to him that the true test of my life isn't whether I succeed or fail. My goal is to give everything I have for what is on my heart. And if I'm pursuing my dream, the results don't matter. I can look back twenty, thirty years from now and say, "I gave everything I had to football, and I gave everything I had to baseball, and I was able to live out some dreams." And in my opinion, that's pretty awesome.

Failure is unavoidable. There is no mission-possible living without tasting the bitter flavor of making a mistake, great or small, or experiencing an undesirable outcome for something you've worked so hard and long for. But if you close your eyes (or hold your nose), you'll find that failure isn't totally unappetizing. Like broccoli, it isn't really that terrible to eat. Failure is how we learn, stretch, and improve. If we want to reach our goals and do what we believe God is calling us to do, we can't be scared of failure. We acknowledge the sweaty palms and heart palpitations, but we don't let them stop us.

Some of the best athletes I've been around failed so many times. They didn't reject the experiences that others might call failures. They didn't pummel themselves with pity or quit. They used those experiences. To them, failure lit an inner fire no one could harness, and ultimately they achieved the goals they set out for.

Failing doesn't make you a failure. It just gives you an opportunity to improve. That's the approach I've lived by. I never want to live with the regret of not trying because I was scared of failing. A key to handling failure so it becomes a friend and not a foe is to change your perspective. This is what experts call reframing.

Say you tried out for a team and didn't make it or you just started your consulting business and haven't had a client in six months. Instead of looking at your present situation and labeling it, or even yourself, as a failure, reframe those negative thoughts. Ask yourself:

- *Is there another way to look at this situation?*
- *What are some reasons this could have happened?*
- *What were some things that stood in my way?*
- *Where do I need to better shift my attention?*

If you plan on doing your best to avoid failure, good luck. Let me know how it goes. We all hope for the best, but we can't control outcomes. And that's a good thing. Embrace failure. If you reframe it as a growth experience, you'll be able to see what you're capable of—which, by the way, is a lot more than you think. And if you live mission possible, you're not going to be stunted by the fear of doing something even if your chances of success are limited.

Think of the last time you experienced failure. What were you trying to do? What happened?

_____

_____

_____

_____

How could you have decided to reframe the failure? What would that look like?

_____

_____

_____

_____

Sickness is a hindrance to the body, but not to your ability to choose, unless that is your choice. Lameness is a hindrance to the leg, but not to your ability to choose. Say this to yourself with regard to everything that happens, then you will see such obstacles as hindrances to something else, but not to yourself.

—EPICTETUS, *The Enchiridion*

Day 28

REMEMBER AND CELEBRATE THE SMALL VICTORIES

UP TO THIS POINT, YOU'VE BEEN WORKING HARD TO live a life full of purpose, meaning, and significance. I'm sure you've encountered obstacles and barriers that have really challenged your commitment to change. But guess what? You've made it this far!

Oftentimes in our pursuits of end goals, we tend to forget the small wins along the way. Usually, when we have a plan—for life, for our careers, for our kids—we place the flag at the finish line and think, *When I get there, I'll celebrate!*

But you know as well as I do that success doesn't happen overnight. Getting to the flag is not always that easy. You don't lose thirty pounds after going to the gym for one week or learn a new language in a month. I always say, championships aren't won in a day; they're won in the off-season, in the weight room, and practice. It takes time to achieve the things you want. Living a mission-possible life is no different. It doesn't happen with the flip of a switch. It's a process of refinery as you face the highs and lows of life. With this being said, it's critical to recognize your progress. It's important to have checkpoints. If you don't, you'll lose confidence and the motivation to keep going.

In my experience, our plans don't always align with reality. I'm sure you can relate!

Tim Ferriss, author of *The 4-Hour Workweek,* once shared in an interview how he used to be terrible at remembering the small wins. He confessed he would often have these big, aggressive, granddaddy goals but would get so worn down in his pursuit to achieve them.

To change this, with the help of his girlfriend, Tim created what he calls the Jar of Awesome. When something really cool or awesome happens, in order to not forget it, he writes it down on a piece of paper, folds it up, and puts it in a large mason jar. Then in times when he's feeling down or in a creative funk, he reaches into his Jar of Awesome and remembers the little successes from the past that got him to where he is now. This principle is super simple and applicable. It's easy to let progress slip our minds. But when you're intentional in tracking your checkpoints, it allows you to stay focused on your destination.

What events in your life are worthy to remember as you pursue mission-possible living? Write down times when you've experienced God's faithfulness or have overcome specific obstacles.

1. _____

_____

2. _____

_____

3. _____

_____

As you reflect on your list, what made these events memorable?

_____

_____

_____

_____

Remembering is only half the victory. Now we get to celebrate.

Jack Welch, CEO of General Electric between 1981 and 2001, was one of the best at commending progress. He ultimately grew General Electric's company valuation from $12 billion to $410 billion.[6] However, it was his personal management style that revolutionized the art of company culture. Considered the top corporate executive and manager of his time,[7] Jack made every effort to acknowledge the small victories within the company. Prior to being CEO, as a general manager of GE's polymer-products division, Jack would celebrate with his team after every tenth order received, after every tenth client acquired, after every internal promotion, after every bonus, and after every raise. As a result, his employees were more energetic and enthusiastic. He firmly believed that the more you celebrate, the better your performance.

Being motivated or encouraged by progress is fundamental to human nature. C'mon, who doesn't want to celebrate? If you want to take your productivity, parenting, business, team, and relationships to the next level, train your brain to focus on progress. No matter how big or small, start to celebrate the wins more often.

Over the past several weeks, have you taken the time to celebrate your growth? If you're new to this, here are some ideas:

- If you can afford it, treat yourself (to coffee, a new outfit, and so on).
- Call a loved one and share your progress.
- Do a happy dance!
- Do something you enjoy that you haven't done in a while (for example, go hiking, read a book, spend a day at the beach).

Identify where you have won or are currently winning in your pursuit of meaning, significance, and purpose.

Q List a recent small win.

A _____

_____

Q How can you celebrate this win?

A _____

_____

Q When will you celebrate this win?

A _____

_____

Whenever you find yourself doubting how far you can go,
just remember how far you have come.

—UNKNOWN

MODULE 6
Build Bridges

A mission-possible life doesn't begin or end with us. Research shows that healthy relationships can help us live longer and manage stress well. I don't know many people who get a pass in life from needing to interact with others.

Let's admit it. We need one another!

For the next five days, let's navigate the messiness many of us encounter in our relationships and learn how to strengthen the right bonds.

Day 29

SEE THE BEST IN OTHERS

HAVE YOU FOUND IT HARD TO LOOK AWAY WHEN passing a car accident? Were you glued to the news at the beginning of the COVID outbreak, unable to stop reading about the increasing numbers of infections and the life-threatening symptoms we were just beginning to learn about? If someone offers you feedback, do you find yourself focusing on that one negative piece of criticism rather than the positive observations?

You aren't alone. This imbalance is called negativity bias. According to basic psychology, the human mind tends to focus on negative things. Most of us remember traumatic experiences better than the happy memories and react more strongly to negative situations than to equally positive ones. For instance, you may have had a pretty good day up until 3 p.m., when you discover that someone posted a sarcastic jab toward you on your social media feed. All of a sudden, that pretty good day detonates. Now all you can think about is that post.

When it comes to relationships, our negativity bias can . . .

- lead us to assume the worst about people.
- be an obstacle to forgiveness.
- magnify people's flaws and mistakes.
- override a person's positive traits.
- ruin relationships.

Though we're hardwired to pay attention to negativity, that doesn't mean we must surrender to living through a negative lens. We have to reroute our focus when our negativity about a person or relationship begins to tip the scales. As much as we can, we must change how we think.

Humans aren't perfect. We are flawed and have baggage. We have hurt and been hurt. Yet we are designed to be relational. We were created to be in relationship with the Creator, first and foremost, and then with others. We need one another. One of the greatest ways we grow as individuals is by nurturing relationships.

Each person is a divine image bearer. Humanity is marked with eternal value, dignity, and worth. Sure, it's easy to get annoyed with a friend, spouse, coworker, or child, but it doesn't have to be our default. We must make an intentional decision to choose to see the best in others rather than focus on whatever negative assumption we have about them or irritating habits we think they have. In other words, notice and say no to your negativity bias.

Here are a few things you can do.

Break the habit. If you find yourself focusing on someone's mistake or failure, list four traits you admire, respect, or like about him or her and redirect your attention in that direction. The more you do this, the more of a habit it becomes.

Pile it on. Consider the impact your negativity has on those around you. If you say something negative to a spouse, child, or friend, say five positive things to him or her over the next few days to balance it out.

Give kindness a chance. In the Bible, God makes it clear that kindness is a big deal: "What is desirable in a person is his kindness" (Proverbs 19:22); "what does the LORD require of you but to do justice, to love kindness, and to walk humbly with your God?" (Micah 6:8). Stamp out negativity with something positive. Give small doses of kindness to those you know and those you encounter throughout your day. Watch how you communicate with others; use positive, affirming words. Be encouraging. Show someone you care by doing something nice for him or her.

In his book *The Seven Principles for Making Marriage Work*, John Gottman proposes an exercise called "I appreciate." Think of five positive characteristics (for example, loyal, hardworking, caring, generous, practical, romantic, consistent, trustworthy) you would use to describe someone close to you who is affected by your negativity bias. The person could be a spouse but doesn't have to be. For each positive characteristic, think of an incident in which this person has demonstrated that characteristic, and write the characteristics and incidents in the appropriate spots below. If you're willing, share with that person what you wrote.

1. Characteristic: _____

Incident: _____

2. Characteristic: _____

Incident: _____

3. Characteristic: _____

Incident: _____

4. Characteristic: _____

Incident: _____

5. Characteristic: _____

Incident: _____

The negativity bias may exist in your mind, but you don't have to allow it to sabotage your relationships. Every day is an opportunity to live mission possible and change your bias, one act at a time.

Kindness is contagious.

—TIM TEBOW

Day 30

FOSTER AN ATTITUDE OF FORGIVENESS

EVER SAY SOMETHING IN THE HEAT OF THE MOMENT that you immediately regret? I have. I try my best to think before I speak so I never have to be in that terrible position, apologizing for words I can't ever unsay. But I've been there.

Many years ago, I was preparing for an event and was not in the best state of mind. I was high on stress and low on sleep. I had an opportunity to chill out behind the scenes and have a moment of reprieve away from people. Someone I didn't know that well was around and started filming me from out of nowhere. Man, I got so angry. I pulled him aside and hissed through clenched teeth, "Dude, what the heck is going on?"

It didn't take long for me to apologize, which was absolutely the right thing for me to do, but I could tell he still held a grudge. I apologized for the second time, with the same amount of sincerity. I felt terrible for what I'd said. Eventually, he forgave me and we both got past this hiccup.

Has that ever happened to you? Maybe you've been the hothead or the one on the receiving end. Perhaps you were under great pressure one season and your spouse made an innocent remark about something and you just lost it on him or her. Or maybe in trying to protect yourself, you became defensive with a friend and made some snide comments that hurt him or her. One thing that's certain is there are plenty of opportunities in this life to hurt and be hurt. Here's what I learned during my anger episode:

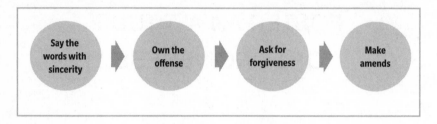

Saying sorry (and meaning it!) is one of the most important acts of humility you can engage in with any relationship. It shows that you care. Speaking aloud and meaning the two words *I'm sorry* is just a start.

After you say the words, be specific and address what you are sorry for. Name the offense and take responsibility for your actions. Then ask for forgiveness. You don't have to grovel at the person's feet or ask them a hundred times, but you should ask for it.

Finally, make amends. See if there is anything you can do, realistically speaking, to repair the damage.

As you read these words, is someone in particular coming to mind? Someone you've hurt or maybe even someone it's time to forgive? Perhaps it's you who needs forgiveness. Spend the next twenty to thirty minutes writing down an apology. If it's you who needs to ask for forgiveness, I encourage you to ask for it. Consider giving the person this letter. If you need to let go of an offense, you can forgive in your heart without the other party asking for forgiveness. You are in charge of liberating yourself.

Take your time. Write about what led to the offense, what happened, how it made you feel both during and afterward, your role in the situation, and what could have been done differently.

It's important to give and accept forgiveness. This might mean forgiving someone for an offense. It might also mean forgiving yourself for something stupid you did. When we hold a grudge or struggle with bitterness because of what someone said or did, we need to check ourselves. Some offenses are easier to move on from than others, no doubt. If you need extra help to process heavier offenses, seek the advice of an expert. A professional can help you sift through your feelings so that you can heal.

It is impossible to live mission possible when we stay stuck in a pattern of unforgiveness. Resisting forgiveness will prevent us from living to our fullest potential and capacity. That's why forgiveness isn't something we should just ask for or receive; it's an attitude we should live with on a daily basis.

Not forgiving is like drinking rat poison
and then waiting for the rat to die.
—ANNE LAMOTT, *Traveling Mercies*

Day 31

TIGHTEN YOUR SQUAD

AMERICAN ENTREPRENEUR AND MOTIVATIONAL speaker Jim Rohn once said that we are the average of the five people we spend the most time with.[1] That may encourage you, if you've surrounded yourself with a stellar squad. But Rohn's words may have the opposite effect on you, especially if this statement triggers the memory of your time in COVID-19 quarantine, when your social sphere was physically limited. As I'm writing this in early February 2021, some states still have certain lockdown measures in place to stop the spread, and I'm hoping by the time this book is released, we'll have moved past the need for social isolation.

Back to Rohn's quote. Think about the five people you spend the most time with. These are not necessarily the people you quarantined with or those you are naturally forced to be around, such as your spouse, roommate, or coworkers. Who are the five people you have chosen to be your friends—the ones you intentionally share your time, energy, emotions, dreams, goals, and experiences with?

Share a little bit about them in the space on the next page. Write down their names, what they mean to you, how they improve your life, how you make them better, and the qualities you admire about them. Finally, write down habits or behavior that you've adopted from them. Maybe you started exercising because a friend introduced you to yoga or you decided to learn a new language due to your wife's encouragement. Or maybe you realize, after reflecting deeply about these relationships, a friend has introduced you to a not-so-great habit, influencing you to loosen some boundaries that you really needed to have set in place. Try to tell the truth, even if it makes you cringe. Just write it down.

1. _____

_____

2. _____

_____

3. _____

_____

4. _____

_____

5. _____

_____

Perhaps you've heard of the social-proximity effect. It's a scientific term that addresses how we become like the people we hang out with the most. It's a natural human response. We tend to mimic what we see. If we observe those closest to us doing or saying certain things, good or bad, the tendency will be, over time, to mirror that behavior. Obviously, if those certain things are positive, awesome! And if not, well, we've got some serious thinking to do.

Out of the five people you listed, are there any relationships that have made it difficult for you to develop as an individual and live a mission-possible life? Maybe it's a friend who questions how much time you spend helping others (and I'm not talking about a healthy, burnout-avoidance line of questioning) and hopes you will spend more time binge-watching reality TV. Or maybe you have a friend who is always questioning your commitment to daily exercise. In the space below, write down specifically how what they do or say impedes your progress.

_____

_____

_____

_____

_____

There may come a time on your journey when you have to reevaluate your relationships. I'm not saying that just because a friend makes a negative comment or is going through a rough season you need to drop that friendship, but stand back for a beat. If those closest to you aren't some of your biggest supporters or cheerleaders of your journey to making your life count, it may be time to tighten your squad.

You need to be intentional not only about how you spend your time in the mission-driven path you are carving out but also about whom you choose to hang out with. Find people who will empower you to change. Choose friends who will believe in you, fire you up, teach you something new, challenge you instead of tell you what you want to hear, encourage you to shift outside what's comfortable, and push you to reach for new heights.

Create a solid support system. Be wise about your top-five list. If someone's bad habits are attracting you in the wrong way, maybe it's time for you to hang out less with that person. When something feels off track, have a conversation with the person and see what you can do to make things right.

Choose your squad wisely, and determine today to be someone who is influenced and who influences in a positive way.

One who walks with wise people will be wise,
but a companion of fools will suffer harm.
—PROVERBS 13:20

Day 32

WHO'S FIGHTING FOR YOU?

AROUND THE SEVENTH CENTURY BC, ANCIENT Greek city-states developed a successful military formation called the phalanx. The phalanx was made up of hoplites, heavy infantry citizen-soldiers who fought when called upon. Each solider was equipped with a spear, a large round wooden shield, a short sword, a helmet, bronze chest armor, and shin gear. When engaging in battle, soldiers would stand in a tight, stacked, shoulder-to-shoulder rectangular position and move forward as one unit. In this formation, their shields would overlap, thus creating a shield wall that made the phalanx nearly impenetrable. When interlocked, the shield would cover not only the soldier's own body but also the right flank of his brother next to him.

The phalanx is considered one of the greatest innovations of military antiquity. Its success relied on discipline and devotion. In head-to-head combat, the soldiers trusted one another to do their job—to cover their backs. If one man got lazy and let down his guard (a.k.a. his shield), his brother in arms would be exposed to danger. Each man wasn't fighting for just himself; he was fighting for the whole group. Depending on where you were placed in the formation, you would always have two to four men on your hip. Through thick and thin, through conquest and setback, the soldiers battled to remain together as one. If separated, the phalanx would fail and suffer defeat. Though small in number, they proved to be an unstoppable force for several centuries.

The truth is we all have blind spots. These areas of weakness make us vulnerable. Just like the ancient Greeks, we need people to fight with us. We cannot do life alone. If a soldier strayed from the group, he would not last long. As you read in day 31, we must find people who will stick with us no matter the circumstance.

What I find most interesting is that the hoplites were just your average ordinary citizens. Yes, they went through specific warrior training, but in times of peace, they were regular dudes with regular jobs. You don't have to be some elite performer, athlete, or entrepreneur to surround yourself with relational protection. Anyone can pull people around them and do life together: coworkers, friends from church, childhood friends, cousins, other family members. These people have the privilege and responsibility to go to war with you.

As we've already discussed in previous modules, life sometimes hits us with the unexpected. I'm sure even since you've started this forty-day journey with me, you've experienced some sort of pain, defeat, or setback. Have you processed this adversity with anybody? I'm here to tell you that if you don't have people on your squad who ask you the direct questions or offer encouragement, you need to find some. If your current squad isn't willing to go to battle with you in the sucky times, maybe you need to reconsider who's in your circle. True accountability happens in the context of relationship.

Be honest with yourself. Do you feel as though you have people in your life who would protect your blind spots? If so, who are they, and how do they keep you accountable?

1. _____

2. _____

3. _____

You need accountability in many different shapes and sizes. Why? Because people see you from different vantage points. A coworker may not see you interact with your family at home, but they sure can keep you healthy and effective at work. Likewise, a best friend may not know the ins and outs of your job, but he or she can definitely check in on how you're loving your wife and kids. Diversify your community. You don't share your deepest, darkest secrets with everyone, so you need different circles.

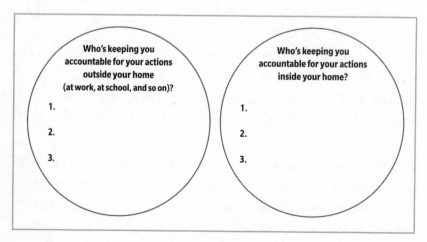

The following is a list of questions you can begin to ask, share, or answer to help guide you in more intentional relationship with those fighting alongside you:

- What areas of life do you feel you're doing well in?
- What areas of life are you falling short in?
- What are you doing to help other people or deepen existing relationships?
- Do you currently have any unhealthy habits that you'd like to change?
- Have you directly or indirectly lied to anyone recently?
- How did you experience joy this week? How did you show kindness this week?
- What are you doing to take care of yourself?

The healthiest relationships are those where you're a team; where you protect each other and stand up for one another.
—SHARON RIVKIN, MA, MFT,
"5 Ways to Become Your Spouse's Best Friend"

Day 33

BE GENUINE WITH PEOPLE

A GOOD FRIEND OF MINE HAD THIS PHRASE THAT he would often repeat to people after conversations or in passing. With a smile on his face, no matter who it was, he would always say, "You're the best. I love you!"

To one person after the other, "You're the best, man. I love you." "Hey, I love you. You're the best!" "Love you, man. Just know, you're the best!"

Trust me—he meant well and had great intentions, because he truly does care for people. He wants to be encouraging, which I love! It just bothered me a bit. Telling every single person the same thing diminishes the value of the statement. In my mind, if everyone is the best, then no one is the best.

We were hanging out once and it came up. I asked him, "Hey, man, if you tell everybody that they're the best and you love them, isn't it that you really told nobody?" A while later, he called me and said, "You know, I've been thinking about what you said. I get it. I want to say what I mean."

Being honest and transparent is not always easy, but it matters. As we build bridges, forming new relationships and going deeper in existing ones, I want to challenge you to be genuine—not only with your actions, but also in how you communicate.

Genuine means actual, real, or true; not false or fake; sincere and honest. More today than ever, I firmly believe in telling people the truth. If we're not being honest with one another, then we're wasting time and energy. I always want those in my circles to know exactly where they stand with me, both in times of praise and in tough conversations. I want to be encouraging but also real. Truthfulness doesn't remove kindness from the equation. But I want people to know that when I say "You did a good job" or "You're the best," I mean it.

Eighteenth-century theologian John Wesley noted, "Let your words be the genuine picture of your heart."[2]

When you speak, do your words reflect how you feel? When you encourage, compliment, and give thanks, are you sharing what's really on your heart, or are you faking it? Write your thoughts here.

_____

_____

_____

_____

See, there are two extremes with genuine communication: speaking your mind with disrespect, or being overly nice and not sharing truth because you don't want to hurt someone's feelings. One extreme is blunt and rude; the other is passive and builds a false sense of confidence. Neither is beneficial.

Just like most things in life, the sweet spot is somewhere in the middle. When you're genuine to others, you want what's best for them. Telling athletes that they played a great game when they really didn't and not giving them feedback on how to improve only hurts them in the long run. As a coach, you want to maximize each player's potential. As a parent, you want to maximize the relationship with each child. As a boss, you want to maximize each employee's performance. Anything less than being genuine hinders growth.

Think about a conversation in which you used the hard truth to share something with someone but it came across as either harsh or insincere. What was the outcome? What could you have done differently?

_____

_____

_____

_____

Being genuine leads to vulnerability, and vulnerability leads to deeper connection.

Practical Ways to Be Genuine

- Be confident in who God says you are.
- Never miss an opportunity to show gratitude.
- Commit to fast, honest, and clear communication.
- Be generous with what you have.
- Show belief in people.

Speak with honesty. Think with sincerity.
Act with integrity.
—UNKNOWN

MODULE 7
Consider Your Character

When you're living for a greater purpose, you must always be looking inward.

Who you are is measured not by who you say you are but rather by what you do, what choices you make, how you treat others, and how you respond to life's unpleasant situations.

In this final module, it's time to look at yourself from the inside out, because living mission possible means more than just doing something nice for someone else; it means getting your priorities aligned and your heart in the right place.

Day 34

BUILD INTEGRITY

BOBBY JONES IS BEST KNOWN FOR BEING THE most successful amateur golfer ever to compete at a national and international level. He is most famous for being the first and only golfer to win a Grand Slam—victory in all four major golf tournaments in a single calendar year, 1930.[1] You might call him something of a legend. Although Jones was acclaimed for his golf skills, he was also lauded for his integrity. The following true story is told about him still, almost a century later.

In the 1925 U.S. Open, Jones was addressing his ball, which lay in the rough. He noticed the ball move as his iron grazed the grass. This would automatically cost him a one-stroke penalty. But here's the thing: no one saw the ball move except Jones. None of the officials—nor his opponent, nor anyone else—had seen the ball move. But because Jones believed it had, he owned up to it and charged himself the penalty. If he hadn't done so, no one would have been the wiser. But Jones knew, and the penalty cost him the win.

When he was praised for his virtuous deed after the fact, Jones was quoted as saying, "You might as well praise me for not robbing banks."[2] I love how humble this legendary golfer was about doing the right thing.

Achieving the goal of making our lives count has a direct relation to what we do in the moments no one is looking and what choices we make when we know we can get away with certain things. A mission-possible life is not only steeped in purpose and significance but also shaped around integrity. What you do in the times no one is looking will reveal your character. Doing the right thing consistently in those moments will build it.

Looking for a simple way to build your integrity? I've got you covered. When I was on the football team in high school, Coach Howard had three team rules. (And they weren't "Catch the pass, tackle someone, and run really hard.") He focused on more than our development as athletes; he also focused on building our character. These were our team rules:

1. Do what's right.

2. Do your best.

3. Treat everybody the way you want to be treated.

These are such great principles to live by. And if you think about it, it's hard not to live mission possible when you follow these three ideas. This doesn't mean we're not going to make mistakes even when we try to do what's right or our best. And there might be times when we have to make choices between two good things or right things and when our best may not align with what someone else thinks our best should be.

That said, these three principles are a great place to start in building your integrity.

Take a few minutes to think about someone you know who you would describe as a person of integrity. What sets her apart from others? What do you admire about her and why? Describe a specific instance where her integrity was called into action. How have you learned from her character? How are you better today for knowing her? Write down the answers to these questions.

_____

_____

_____

_____

_____

_____

_____

Integrity is essential for living with significance and living mission possible. Take inventory of your actions, particularly during the moments you are alone, and evaluate the quality of your character.

Ways to Model Integrity

- Keep appointments.
- Show up on time.
- Keep your word.
- Lead by example.
- Accept responsibility for your actions.
- Fulfill your promises.
- Treat others with respect.
- Be open, honest, and fair in your communication.
- Admit when you are wrong.
- Exercise self-control.
- Keep it positive.

Integrity is doing the right thing
no matter what it costs you.

—CHARLES W. MARSHALL, *Shattering the Glass Slipper*

Day 35

DEAL WITH DISAPPOINTMENT

I AM INSPIRED BY WINSTON CHURCHILL, MOST REC-ognized for his stellar leadership during World War II. Even people who aren't history buffs know his name and are familiar with his inspiring speeches that rallied allegiance and pride among those he served. His words continue to resonate beyond his own country and among future generations.

A lesser-known fact about Churchill is the disastrous military campaign he led earlier in his career called the Battle of Gallipoli. During the First World War, he came up with a plan to seize control of the Dardanelles Strait. This would provide the Allies with advantages for them to attack Constantinople, the capital of Turkey at the time, and force the Ottoman Empire out of the war. But the campaign failed, and tens of thousands of Allied lives were lost. The blame was hurled at Churchill. In response, he was demoted to the lowest seat in the cabinet. To say he was disappointed is an understatement. His wife, Clementine, lamented of her husband's failure, "The Dardanelles haunted him for the rest of his life. He always believed in it. When he left the Admiralty he thought he was finished. I thought he would never get over the Dardanelles; I thought he would die of grief."[3]

Not long after his demotion, Churchill resigned from his cabinet position and joined the war in France as an infantry officer. Here's what he didn't do. He didn't give up his dream of making a difference in politics. He didn't turn his back on his country. He didn't stop serving the men and women he believed in. He took time to reflect and to reframe his disappointment as a learning opportunity, all while serving his country and others.

Each one of us has experienced disappointment, whether we've been rejected, overlooked, undervalued, or weighed down by the haunting repercussions of failure. I've had my fair share of disappointing experiences, some of which you may have already read or heard about, whether it was getting cut or seeing people who promised to fight for me break that promise.

When we are sucker punched with disappointment, it can embitter us and create a lingering sadness that stunts forward movement of any kind. But it can also ignite within us a stronger resilience and forge robust growth. Some people process disappointment better than others. It's an individual thing. I'm sure you know someone who is quick to get over things and someone who isn't.

Although disappointment is real and affects each of us differently, we don't have to be controlled by its negative force. Being chained by it will not allow us to dream big or believe we can make a difference or make us want to serve others. I'm not naive enough to tell you to just get over a disappointing situation, but here are a few things you can do to help beat the feeling of disappointment, one step at a time.

1. **Shift your language.** Instead of negative self-talk, try positive speech. Instead of telling yourself, *This is so bad. My life is over,* try thinking, *I will regroup and try something different next time.*

2. **Work on a new goal.** Set out to achieve something you've always wanted to do. Accomplishing something, even small, will boost your confidence.

3. **Do something nice for someone else.** Get that helper's high we talked about in day 18. It's a mood adjuster, for sure!

4. **Reframe the disappointment.** Instead of allowing your emotions to lead, reflect on the situation in an unbiased way. What could you have done better, different, sooner, or later? Get some feedback. Use the experience as a learning tool.

You may have encountered disappointment on your journey, but it doesn't have to define your destiny or legacy. Use the questions below to reflect on how you've handled disappointment in your life.

Q List two major disappointments you've experienced.

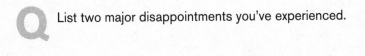

A _____

_____

Q Why were they disappointments?

A _____
_____

Based on what you wrote, how might you have used one or more of the tips mentioned earlier to process through the disappointment?

1. _____

2. _____

We must accept finite disappointment,
but never lose infinite hope.
—MARTIN LUTHER KING JR.

Day 36

SELF-DISCIPLINE
AS GRATITUDE

THE WORD *DISCIPLINE* MAY MAKE YOU WINCE OR bring to mind memories of punishment, but there is more to it. *Discipline* can be traced back to the fourteenth century from the Latin word *disciplina*, which means "instruction given, teaching, learning, knowledge"; in 1500, it came to take on a more militaristic tone: "training to follow orders and act in accordance with rules."[4] The word today can mean all those things.

Living a mission-possible life requires discipline. I think of discipline as a hybrid of self-training to improve and grow in character as well as self-leadership to turn the "want to" in your life into actionable steps. Self-discipline is the commitment to focus on what's most important to you rather than what you'd really want right now. It surpasses motivation in that it's not just an urge to do something; it is the grit to actually go out and do it. We might reframe self-discipline as a way to love ourselves. That's a pretty cool way of looking at it. If we love the masterpiece the Creator has made, self-discipline is a way of honoring and caring for that masterpiece. Not only is it a way of loving ourselves, but it is also an expression of gratitude. When we leverage the art of self-discipline by creating good habits as we make our lives count, it is a way of thanking God for who He is and what He has done.

Discipline isn't a bad or dirty word. Jim Rohn (who was mentioned in day 31) called discipline a bridge between goals and accomplishments. Growing up, I tacked a quote on my bedroom wall that said, "Somewhere he is out there training while I am not, and when we meet, he will win."[5] I got this quote from a commercial I watched in the 1990s that showed kids around the world shooting free throws. The thirty-second clip inspired me to get up and do something when someone else wasn't.

I believe in being the best you can at whatever you do. If you're a parent, a teacher, graphic designer, musician, or physician, crush it. Don't do merely an okay job or just get by. Do everything with excellence. Stand out. Do things a little differently. Get up earlier. Stay up later. Study harder. Train better. Working at being your best, making the most out of whatever God has given you, is your way of thanking Him.

One of the most basic ways to gauge your self-discipline is to take a look at the fundamentals. How are you taking care of yourself when it comes to sleep, nutrition, and exercise? Are you eating nutrient-dense foods and drinking enough water? Are you getting at least seven hours of uninterrupted sleep at night? Do you get regular exercise most days of the week? To be your best requires taking care of yourself at a basic level. Take some time to evaluate your health habits in these three areas.

Write down one goal you'd like to achieve in each area (for example, sleep seven hours, eat more fruits and vegetables, and exercise more), and then list two specific action steps that you will commit to each day for the next thirty days to begin to up your self-discipline game (for example, sleep seven hours per night, go to bed an hour early each night, read instead of watching movies before bed).

Category	Goal	Action Steps
Sleep	_____	_____
Nutrition	_____	_____
Exercise	_____	_____

The price of excellence is discipline.
The cost of mediocrity is disappointment.
—WILLIAM ARTHUR WARD, *Thoughts of a Christian Optimist*

Day 37

LET YOUR YES BE YES

WE ALL HAVE THAT ONE FRIEND, FAMILY MEMBER, or coworker who's not the greatest at keeping commitments. He says one thing but does another or doesn't follow through. Maybe he forgot about a lunch date or is regularly late to meetings or cancels plans at the last minute. If only it happened just once in a while. But it doesn't. This person has a habit of not keeping his word.

Unfortunately, the reality is that we are all guilty of this flakiness, at one time or another. And we probably do it more often than we think. It's easy to point a finger. We can make lists of people who have wronged us in some way, but I'm sure you're on someone's list as well. Whether we fall short due to the desire to please people or struggle with FOMO (fear of missing out), our character is on the line every time we make a commitment. When we don't fulfill our commitments, our character is in question.

That's why it's so critical to let your yes mean yes. Translation: when you say you're going to do something, do it.

John D. Rockefeller Jr., the son of the wealthy oil titan John D. Rockefeller, said, "I believe in the sacredness of a promise, that a man's word should be as good as his bond; that character—not wealth or power or position—is of supreme worth."[6] I love that! The Rockefellers were sticklers for truth. Father and son both instilled the principles of honesty and integrity into their employees. No matter how much money they made (and they made *a lot*), they wanted to be men of their word.

When you don't keep your word, you lose credibility. When you commit to something and don't follow through, you show others that you cannot be trusted. If you say you're going to do something, then do it. Don't make excuses. Don't make other plans. Don't be late. Follow through. This is part of building trust with yourself and other people.

And I know life happens. I'm not talking about the times when last-minute emergencies come up. I'm talking about the pattern of not living up to the expectations we set. That is when it's the norm, not the exception. Essentially, when we don't keep our word, we're saying, *My time, my wants, my needs, and my busy schedule are more important than you. I respect myself more than I respect you. I value me more than I value you.* And that's not right.

Making a commitment means sticking with it, even when we don't feel like it. It's so easy to commit to things loosely. We like the freedom and flexibility to get out of something if there's a better option. We want to do what's convenient for us at the time.

If you tell your coach you'll show up before practice to run extra drills, you better be there. If you tell your friend who's struggling with a stressful situation to call you at a specific time, you better be available when he or she calls. Worst-case scenario, you shoot the person a quick text explaining why you'll be running late or can't make it. When you do this, you demonstrate thought, kindness, and consideration.

Do you tend to trust promises or react with skepticism? Why?

_____

_____

_____

_____

Do you ever find yourself wondering, *Why can't [name of person] be on time?* or *Why don't they just let me know sooner if they need to cancel?* Maybe you're that person. Are you known for not following through? What changes do you need to make?

_____

_____

_____

_____

As the saying goes, people with good intentions make promises, but people with good character keep them.

> *Don't say anything you don't mean. . . . Just say "yes" and "no." When you manipulate words to get your own way, you go wrong.*
> —MATTHEW 5:33, 37, MSG

Day 38

THE POWER OF HUMILITY

WHEN I PLAYED FOOTBALL AT THE UNIVERSITY OF Florida, our team was blessed to win a national championship in my freshman and junior years. I also won a Heisman Trophy in my sophomore year. During my senior year, our goal was to win another national championship.

That year, we had a great season. We went undefeated, 12–0. We were the defending national champs and all year long were ranked the number one college team in the country. When we got to the SEC Championship Game, we played Alabama and lost. Everything that we'd been working for fell apart in three hours. It didn't take away all our past success, but I was very disappointed.

That entire next week was a miserable one for me. Most people who know me know that I'm very competitive, and I think that time I let it go too far. I stayed in a funk for a few days. The weekend after that game, the Home Depot College Football Awards was held in Orlando, Florida. I knew I was probably not going to win anything, so I wasn't super excited to be there.

The night before, my family and I walked into a restaurant for an event relating to the awards ceremony. There I was introduced to a young woman named Kelly Faughnan. Little did I know how much Kelly would affect my life for years to come.

I'll never forget watching her walk toward me. I saw how hard it was for her to take each step. I'd learn that she had multiple brain tumors that affected how her entire body functioned. When we reached each other, she gave me a great big hug and squeezed with such strength. She started crying, which made me cry, and then her family started crying, which made my family cry—and no one had even said a word yet!

As Kelly and I were chatting, she began to tell me her story—what she'd been fighting and how she'd persevered. I was greatly moved and humbled. I had been so focused on myself that I'd lost sight of others. Immediately, I felt it was put on my heart to ask her to be my date the next night for the red carpet and the awards show. Thankfully, she said yes! The morning of the awards, my uncle Bill bought Kelly a beautiful dress. She looked stunning. We had an early dinner before the awards ceremony and enjoyed walking down the red carpet. I believe I was up for six awards. When the show started and they announced the first award and I lost, I thought, *It's okay. It's not a big deal. Tonight's about Kelly.* They announced the next award and I lost. That stung a little bit, but no problem. They announced the third award and I lost. Fourth award, nothing. Fifth award, same. At that point, I was frustrated. I started to slide down a self-centered rabbit hole, where it was all about me.

My mom was sitting behind me, and she could tell I was struggling. She leaned over, tapped me on the shoulder, and whispered in my ear, "You've already won tonight. You just don't get your reward until heaven."

Today I can't even remember what awards I was up for. My mom was right. I had won the night! Not because I had received a metal trophy, but because Kelly reminded me of what's most important: people. Kelly helped me gain perspective, which helped me gain humility. The night wasn't about me; it truly was about Kelly.

See, humility is not thinking less of yourself; it's thinking about yourself less. It is truly liberating to sit back and think, *It's not all about me.* It's amazing to remember that on that evening in Orlando, God placed me inside that banquet hall to meet Kelly, to spend such memorable time with her and her family, and to get to know a person who's fought bigger and harder battles than I ever will.

When we humble ourselves, our focus shifts from our personal wants to what really matters, such as fulfilling the needs of others. And that is exactly what Jesus did for each one of us.

Do you have a story of when you've been humbled? In the space below, take some time to remember the power in putting other people first.

_____

_____

_____

_____

_____

Q Whose needs can you put above your own this week?

A Name: _____

_____

Q How will you do this?

A Name: _____

_____

Humility is the virtue that sustains a relationship.

—JEFF BROWN,

pastor of local outreach, College Park Church

POSTLUDE

Bring It Home

Congratulations! You've almost reached the finish line. My prayer is that you've learned and been inspired and challenged much. Let's run together these last two days and bring it home.

Day 39

PUT IT ALL TOGETHER

WELL, HERE WE ARE, ALMOST AT THE END OF FORTY days of Christ-driven, others-focused, and purpose-minded discovery that will catapult you into living a mission-possible life. You've learned how to get out of your own way and into a life of purpose.

In **Module 1, Unlock Your Purpose,** you learned that purpose on a macro scale is about glorifying God and furthering His kingdom. On a micro level, it's about doing those things using our own gifts, talents, skills, and even seasons.

In **Module 2, Pursue Your Passion,** you discovered the true meaning of passion and the depth of its essence. You learned about the importance of having an open spirit, creating awareness, and being teachable as you pursue what you are willing to sacrifice for.

In **Module 3, Get Comfortable Being Uncomfortable,** I reminded you of the value of discomfort—that being uncomfortable is something to be embraced rather than avoided. You began to see adversity not just as obstacles but as opportunities for growth and gaining new ground in your character, experience, and fortitude.

In **Module 4, Get Locked In,** you recognized the gravity of a distraction-free space. You were made painfully aware of how much time you waste when you are not mindful about harnessing your attention. You realized mission-possible living is possible only if you show up, focus, and finish what you start.

In **Module 5, Strain and Strive,** you dug deep into mission-possible living and began to recognize the difference between living for material success and striving for eternal significance. You've pushed mediocrity out of your vocabulary and reframed failure as a positive road leading to greener pastures. You've learned how to conjure inner grit and propel forward into a future in which you can create lasting change.

In **Module 6, Build Bridges,** you reached outward and focused on the importance of relationships. No man or woman is an island, right? You were encouraged to see the best in others, continually foster an attitude of forgiveness, and lock arms with a solid support network.

In **Module 7, Consider Your Character,** you took time to reflect and assess your reaction and response in critical times. You developed thick character that can sustain temptation and disappointment.

Now, go back to each module and look at some of the notes you jotted down, phrases and sentences you highlighted, and insights you've learned. Remind yourself of what struck you most, and write it down here or in a separate journal.

_____

_____

_____

_____

_____

_____

_____

_____

_____

_____

_____

_____

_____

Reading and writing and journaling are wonderful things to do, but what makes a mission-possible life possible is actually living it out. Review the highlights of our time together, and tomorrow you're going to have an opportunity to commit to changing your existence into a mission-possible way of living.

It's not about standing still and becoming safe. If anybody wants to keep creating, they have to be about change.
—MILES DAVIS

Day 40

PLAN FOR PURPOSE

COMMITTING TO CHANGE ALLOWS US TO TAKE action with ourselves and others. This change can begin only after we take responsibility. A mission-possible life isn't a place you magically appear in after clicking your heels three times. Instead, a mission-possible life involves choosing to put your trust in the Creator and being intentional in how you live each day.

If right now you feel a little overwhelmed about making adjustments to your habits, relationships, and outlooks and don't know where to start, I'm here to help.

Over the next few pages, you'll find what I'm calling a Plan for Purpose. This two-part exercise will help you identify how to move forward. The check-in is just a series of questions to pinpoint specific areas that may need closer attention. (Perhaps some of them you have highlighted in yesterday's assignment.) The checkup will help you follow up on the strides you have made or where you may need to course-correct. This is something you can do as often as you'd like. I'm including a Plan for Purpose for one week, one month, and one year. Focus on as many areas in your life as you'd like to; just make sure your many choices aren't so overwhelming that you feel frozen, unsure of where to begin. Be ambitious but also realistic.

One final note: Find an accountability partner to check in with and check up with who will support and challenge you when you need it most. This can be a friend, mentor, or coach.

Plan for Purpose (One Week)

Check-In

1. Over the next week, what specific aspect of your life needs your attention in order to make your life count (for example, physical health, emotional dysfunction, a bad habit, and so on).

_____

_____

2. What is the purpose behind this change?

_____

_____

3. In order to change these behaviors, dysfunctions, or habits, what do you need to be honest about with yourself and with God?

_____

_____

4. List the action steps that will help you make this change.

_____

_____

5. Who will help you persist in your plan this week?

_____

_____

Checkup

1. What progress did you make on your Plan for Purpose this past week?

_____

_____

2. What did you learn about yourself or someone else through this plan?

_____

_____

3. List three key items you'd like to remember from this past week:

- _____
- _____
- _____

Plan for Purpose (One Month)

Check-In

1. Over the next month, what specific aspect of your life needs your attention in order to make your life count (for example, physical health, emotional dysfunction, a bad habit, and so on).

_____

_____

2. What is the purpose behind this change?

_____

_____

3. In order to change these behaviors, dysfunctions, or habits, what do you need to be honest about with yourself and with God?

_____

_____

4. List the action steps that will help you make this change.

_____

_____

5. Who will help you persist in your plan this month?

_____

_____

Checkup

1. What progress did you make on your Plan for Purpose this past month?

_____

_____

2. What did you learn about yourself or someone else through this plan?

_____

_____

3. List three key items you'd like to remember from this past month:

- _____
- _____
- _____

Plan for Purpose (One Year)

Check-In

1. Over the next year, what specific aspect of your life needs your attention in order to make your life count (for example, physical health, emotional dysfunction, a bad habit, and so on).

_____

_____

2. What is the purpose behind this change?

_____

_____

3. In order to change these behaviors, dysfunctions, or habits, what do you need to be honest about with yourself and with God?

_____

_____

4. List the action steps that will help you make this change.

_____

_____

5. Who will help you persist in your plan this year?

_____

_____

Checkup

1. What progress did you make on your Plan for Purpose this past year?

_____

_____

2. What did you learn about yourself or someone else through this plan?

_____

_____

3. List three key items you'd like to remember from this past year:

- _____
- _____
- _____

A FINAL WORD

Dear Reader,

    I am so honored to have been able to spend the past forty (or more) days with you. I truly, from the bottom of my heart, believe that you are created to live a mission-possible life. I'm grateful that you have chosen to begin this journey, and I can't wait to hear some of the amazing adventures I hope you will share with me. Know there will be ups and downs, but through every twist and turn, you still remain on a mission to make your life count. You've got this!

Tim

NOTES

Prelude: Prepare for What's to Come

1. Tyler Gray, "Oscar-Nominated 'Waste Land' Examines Recycling Through the Eyes of Brazil's Dump Denizens," *Fast Company*, October 26, 2010, www.fastcompany.com/1698070/oscar-nominated -waste-land-examines-recyling-through-eyes-brazils-dump-denizens.
2. Gray, "Oscar-Nominated 'Waste Land.'"
3. Winston Churchill, "We Shall Fight on the Beaches," speech, June 4, 1940, House of Commons, London, https://winstonchurchill.org/ resources/speeches/1940-the-finest-hour/we-shall-fight-on-the -beaches.
4. Alice, "Your State's Most-Searched Phobia | 2020," Security Center, October 12, 2020, www.yourlocalsecurity.com/blog/2020-each-states -phobia.
5. Kaya Burgess, "Speaking in Public Is Worse Than Death for Most," *Times*, October 30, 2013, www.thetimes.co.uk/article/speaking-in -public-is-worse-than-death-for-most-5l2bvqlmbnt.

Module 1: Unlock Your Purpose

1. For more on the Great Fire of London, see "Great Fire of London Begins," History, www.history.com/this-day-in-history/great-fire-of -london-begins.
2. For one telling of this common story of three bricklayers, see https:// sacredstructures.org/mission/the-story-of-three-bricklayers-a -parable-about-the-power-of-purpose.
3. Tim Tebow Foundation, www.timtebowfoundation.org/ministries.

4. Benjamin Franklin, quoted in Chris Good, "Picture of the Day: Benjamin Franklin's Daily Schedule," *Atlantic*, April 20, 2011, www .theatlantic.com/politics/archive/2011/04/picture-of-the-day -benjamin-franklins-daily-schedule/237615.

Module 2: Pursue Your Passion

1. Dictionary.com, s.v. "passion," www.dictionary.com/browse/passion.
2. Tara Bahrampour, "Why 'Find Your Passion' Is Bad Advice," *Seattle Times*, August 20, 2018, www.seattletimes.com/explore/careers/why -find-your-passion-is-bad-advice.
3. Wiktionary, s.v. "passion," https://en.wiktionary.org/wiki/passion; "Bathos, Pathos—and Passion," Glossophilia, March 30, 2019, www .glossophilia.org/2019/03/bathos-pathos-and-passion.
4. "Bridger Wilderness," Forest Service: United States Department of Agriculture, www.fs.usda.gov/recarea/btnf/recarea/?recid=77360.
5. Park comments, April 17, 1997, www.radford.edu/~ibarland//Public/ Humor/parkComments.
6. Susan Jeffers, *Feel the Fear . . . and Do It Anyway* (New York: Ballantine, 2006).
7. Bible Hub, s.v. "musar," https://biblehub.com/hebrew/4148.htm.
8. Alex Honnold, quoted in Mark Synnott, "Legendary Climber Alex Honnold Shares His Closest Call," *National Geographic*, December 30, 2015, www.nationalgeographic.com/adventure/adventure-blog/2015/ 12/30/ropeless-climber-alex-honnolds-closest-call/#close.

Module 3: Get Comfortable Being Uncomfortable

1. Daeyeol Lee, quoted in "Aren't Sure? Brain Is Primed for Learning," *Yale News*, July 19, 2018, https://news.yale.edu/2018/07/19/arent-sure -brain-primed-learning; Jessica Stillman, "Science Has Just Confirmed That If You're Not Outside Your Comfort Zone, You're Not Learning," *Inc.*, August 14, 2018, www.inc.com/jessica -stillman/want-to-learn-faster-make-your-life-more-unpredictable .html.
2. Auren Hoffman, quoted in Jessica Stillman, "You Should Spend 70 Percent of Your Time Doing Hard Things, Says This 5-Time Entrepre-

neur," *Inc.*, July 19, 2018, www.inc.com/jessica-stillman/follow-70
-percent-rule-to-maximize-learning-says-this-5x-entrepreneur.html.

3. Hoffman, "70 Percent of Your Time."

4. Mother Teresa, quoted in Fady Noun, "Mother Teresa, the War in Lebanon and the Rescue of 100 Orphans and Children with Disabilities," AsiaNews.it, September 2, 2016, www.asianews.it/news-en/Mother-Teresa%2C-the-war-in-Lebanon-and-the-rescue-of-100-orphans-and-children-with-disabilities-38470.html.

5. Mother Teresa, quoted in Gerald Nadler, "Mother Teresa Leads Crippled Children from West Beirut," *United Press International*, August 14, 1982, www.upi.com/Archives/1982/08/14/Mother-Teresa-leads-crippled-childen-from-west-Beirut/6869398145600.

6. Erik Weihenmayer, "Success Without Seeing: How Erik Weihenmayer Climbed Everest and Kayaked the Grand Canyon Blind," YouTube video, 53:55, from *School of Greatness* podcast, episode 487, posted by "Lewis Howes," May 21, 2017, www.youtube.com/watch?v=sNsifOL-ncc&t=1138s.

7. Larry Dossey, "The Helper's High," *ScienceDirect*, www.sciencedirect.com/science/article/pii/S1550830718304178.

Module 4: Get Locked In

1. Angela Duckworth, quoted in Jeremy Engle, "Are You Easily Distracted?," *New York Times*, October 15, 2020, www.nytimes.com/2020/10/15/learning/are-you-easily-distracted.html.

2. Kevin McSpadden, "You Now Have a Shorter Attention Span Than a Goldfish," *Time*, May 14, 2015, https://time.com/3858309/attention-spans-goldfish.

3. Matthew A. Killingsworth and Daniel T. Gilbert, "A Wandering Mind Is an Unhappy Mind," *Science* 330, November 12, 2010, https://wjh-www.harvard.edu/~dtg/KILLINGSWORTH%20&%20GILBERT%20(2010).pdf.

4. Amishi Jha, "The Science of Taming the Wandering Mind," *Mindful*, June 16, 2017, www.mindful.org/taming-the-wandering-mind.

5. Vicky Valet, "Working from Home During the Coronavirus Pandemic: What You Need to Know," *Forbes*, March 12, 2020, www.forbes.com/sites/vickyvalet/2020/03/12/working-from-home-during-the-coronavirus-pandemic-what-you-need-to-know.

6. John Kotter, *A Sense of Urgency* (Boston: Harvard Business, 2008), 6–7.

7. Dictionary.com, s.v. "consistency," www.dictionary.com/browse/consistence.

8. Stephen Yost, "A Complete Guide to Understanding the Tour de France," *Men's Journal*, www.mensjournal.com/adventure/a-complete-guide-to-understanding-the-tour-de-france.

9. Paul Knott, "Team Sky's Tour de France Rest Day Routine Revealed," *Cycling Weekly*, July 11, 2016, www.cyclingweekly.com/news/racing/team-skys-rest-day-routine-revealed-258405.

Module 5: Strain and Strive

1. Daniel Cappello, "The Better Doctor," *New Yorker*, November 28, 2004, www.newyorker.com/magazine/2004/12/06/the-better-doctor.

2. "Roger Bannister: First Sub-Four-Minute Mile," Guinness World Records, www.guinnessworldrecords.com/records/hall-of-fame/first-sub-four-minute-mile.

3. Roger Bannister, quoted in "Roger Bannister: First Sub-Four-Minute Mile."

4. Peter Vigneron, "Last in the First: An Oral History of the First Sub-4:00 Mile," *Tracksmith*, www.tracksmith.com/journal/article/last-in-the-first-an-oral-history-of-the-first-sub-400-mile.

5. Stephen A. Smith, quoted in Samuel Smith, "Tim Tebow Defends His Baseball Dream in Interview with ESPN Critic Stephen A. Smith," *Christian Post*, October 26, 2016, www.christianpost.com/news/tim-tebow-defends-baseball-dream-interview-espn-critic-stephen-a-smith-watch.html.

6. Marty Steinberg, "Jack Welch, Former Chairman and CEO of GE, Dies at 84," CNBC, March 2, 2020, www.cnbc.com/2020/03/02/jack-welch-obit-ge.html.

7. Claudio Fernández-Aráoz, "Jack Welch's Approach to Leadership," *Harvard Business Review*, March 3, 2020, https://hbr.org/2020/03/jack-welchs-approach-to-leadership.

Module 6: Build Bridges

1. Jim Rohn, quoted in Aimee Groth, "You're the Average of the Five People You Spend the Most Time With," *Insider*, July 24, 2012, www
.businessinsider.com/jim-rohn-youre-the-average-of-the-five-people
-you-spend-the-most-time-with-2012-7.

2. John Wesley, "The Sermons of John Wesley: Sermon 24: Upon Our Lord's Sermon on the Mount: Discourse Four," The Wesley Center Online, http://wesley.nnu.edu/john-wesley/the-sermons-of-john
-wesley-1872-edition/sermon-24-upon-our-lords-sermon-on-the
-mount-discourse-four.

Module 7: Consider Your Character

1. J. E. Luebering, "Bobby Jones: American Golfer," *Britannica*, www
.britannica.com/biography/Bobby-Jones.

2. Bobby Jones, quoted in Ethan Trex, "Fun and Sick Facts About U.S. Open," CNN, June 12, 2008, www.cnn.com/2008/LIVING/wayoflife/
06/12/us.open.history/index.html.

3. John Lee, "Winston Churchill and the First World War," International Churchill Society, 2017, https://winstonchurchill.org/publications/
finest-hour-extras/churchill-first-world-war.

4. Online Etymology Dictionary, s.v. "discipline (*n.*)," www.etymonline
.com/word/discipline.

5. Paraphrased from Dr. Gabe Mirkin, "Tom Fleming, Marathoner Who Out-Trained Everyone Else," DrMirkin.com, April 13, 2017, www
.drmirkin.com/histories-and-mysteries/tom-flleming-marathoner
-who-outtrained-everyone-else.html.

6. John D. Rockefeller Jr., "The Credo of John D. Rockefeller Jr.," Brown Library, https://library.brown.edu/create/rock50/the-credo-of-john-d
-rockefeller-jr.

PHOTO © ADAM SZARMACK, MISSION DRIVEN STUDIOS

TIM TEBOW is a two-time national champion, Heisman Trophy winner, first-round NFL draft pick, and a former professional baseball player. Tebow currently serves as a speaker, is a college football analyst with ESPN and the SEC Network, and is the author of four *New York Times* bestsellers, including *Shaken, This Is the Day,* and the children's book *Bronco and Friends: A Party to Remember.* He is the founder and leader of the Tim Tebow Foundation (TTF), whose mission is to bring faith, hope, and love to those needing a brighter day in their darkest hour of need. Tim is married to Demi-Leigh Tebow (née Nel-Peters), a speaker, influencer, entrepreneur, and Miss Universe 2017. Tim and Demi live in Jacksonville, Florida, with their three dogs, Chunk, Kobe, and Paris.

www.timtebow.com
Facebook, Instagram, Twitter: @timtebow
LinkedIn: www.linkedin.com/in/timtebow15
TikTok: @timtebow_15

ALSO AVAILABLE!

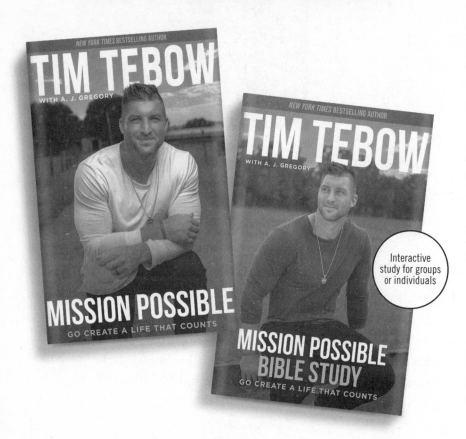

TimTebow.com/MissionPossible